PERSIAN COOKING
FOR A HEALTHY KITCHEN

By

N A J M I E H   K H A L I L I   B A T M A N G L I J

MAGE PUBLISHERS
WASHINGTON, D.C.
1994

To the memory of my sister, Afkham Atri

Copyright ©1994 by Najmieh Batmanglij

Book design by Najmieh Batmanglij

Library of Congress Cataloging-in-Publication Data

Batmanglij, Najmieh,
Persian Cooking for a Healthy Kitchen/by Najmieh Khalili Batmanglij—1st ed.
p. cm.
Includes index.
ISBN 0-934211-40-X
1. Cookery, Iranian. 2. Low-fat diet—Recipes. I. Title
TX725.I7B374 1994
641.5955—dc20

First Edition

Printed and manufactured in
the United States of America

Mage books are available through independent bookstores
or directly from the publisher toll free (800) 962-0922 or (202) 342-1642

CONTENTS

PREFACE

I found my way to this book by a roundabout route. When my husband and I were living in southern France in the early 1980s, the countryside, the crooked streets, the broken tiles, the perfume of wisteria and jasmine, the captivating kitchen aromas of onions, garlic and parsley all summoned back memories of my childhood in Iran and inspired me to write a cookbook in French, *Ma Cuisine d'Iran*. Later, we moved to America, and I wrote a cookbook in English, *Food of Life: Ancient Persian and Modern Iranian Cooking and Ceremonies,* and then a successor volume, *New Food of Life,* which included samplings of Persian literature and miniatures as a cultural backdrop for the recipes.

France remained part of our lives. We continued to spend part of the year at our house in Vence, and those months always re-awakened memories of the beautiful aspects of Persian culture and traditions: the poetry, music, markets and bazaars; the rose gardens and fountains; the orchards of pomegranate and quince; the intoxicating perfume of Seville orange groves in blossom; the magic of old persimmon trees in autumn. Similarities between the Iran of old and the villages of southern France are many—not just the crooked streets and the aromas but also the temperament of the people and the styles and ingredients of the cuisines. As for America, it affected my cooking interests as well, especially with the shift toward lighter, healthier eating styles. I found myself becoming more and more conscious of the fat content of Persian food.

Although Persian food is one of the oldest cooking traditions in the world, it is little known in America. This is less true of France, as my husband and I discovered when we first visited the restaurants of such heralded young chefs as Roger Vergé and Alain Ducas. I was amazed when one day I saw a traditional Persian dish, Sheep's Head and Trotters Soup, on Alain Ducas' menu at the Terrasse of the Juana Hotel. (He is now a Grand Chef in Monte Carlo.) It came with a mixed vegetable pickle, *torshi,* which is exactly how it is served in Iran. When I spoke to him about it and commented on his use of a fresh sprig of mint as a garnish for many dishes, he said, "Of course I have been influenced by Middle Eastern cooking." Recently, in a gourmet market in Washington, D.C., I noticed quince and rose-petal jams with Roger Vergé's label on the jars. In all candor, I must say that my quince and rose-petal jams are better. Why look to France for the secrets of ancient Persian cooking? Go to the cultural sources.

This book draws on my 15 years of researching Persian traditions, collecting recipes, and presenting authentic Persian food and ceremonies in books, articles, lectures and cooking classes. But it is also a new road for me. The purpose of what follows is to modernize—to adapt Persian recipes to today's low-fat, high-flavor eating styles.

The foundation for much of Persian cooking is rice. When rice is combined with a little fish, fowl or meat, plenty of onion, garlic, vegetables, fruit, nuts and herbs, and a delicate mix of spices such as rose petals, dried limes, candied orange peels, cinnamon, cardamom, cumin and saffron, the result is a dish both healthy and uniquely Persian—as colorful as a miniature, exotic yet simple like a poem by Omar Khayyam.

All the recipes for the main dishes fall within the current health goal of limiting calories from saturated fats to 25 percent of one's total food intake. For sautéing and frying, I have used olive oil instead of butter. For dairy products, I have used low-fat varieties: low-fat milk, yogurt and whey. The presentation of the recipes in the photographs is the result of my collaboration with Thierry Jeanneret, a young and very talented French chef at the Belles Rives hotel in Juan les Pins. He was interested in knowing more about the use of spices in Persian cooking, and I wanted a contemporary look for the presentation of Persian food. Not all Persian recipes could be adapted to meet my criteria of low-fat and high-flavor, but each of the 95 recipes in this book works, and works well. They have all been tested by both Iranian and American chefs. In fact, I have been using only these recipes at home for the past two years. Initially worried that my husband and younger son, both "butter men," would complain, I would add butter to their plates separately, but for the past year I have not been doing that and they have not been complaining.

In Persian cooking, every herb and spice is viewed as having its own nutritional and pharmacological properties. I have tried to remain faithful to the original herbs and spices used by my mother and her mother before her. Since ancient times, saffron has been renowned for salubrious and aphrodisiac powers; cumin seeds are said to reduce stomach gas, rose petals and rose water to relieve stomach upsets. Barberries have been used for thousands of years to lower blood pressure and, in juice form, to cleanse the system. Seville orange peels are believed to aid digestion. Verjuice (juice of the unripe grape) is an ancient remedy for rheumatism. Angelica seeds (*gol-par,* which in Persian means the flower of angels) are appropriately thought to have angelic healing powers.

But ultimately, cooking is about sharing, not making, and if these recipes are prepared with love, you too will indeed share their magic.

The French would say *Bon Appétit,* but in Persian we say *Nush-e jan:* Enjoy this food of life.

Najmieh Batmanglij
Georgetown, February 1994

Low-Fat Yogurt

**2 quarts low-fat milk, 2% milk fat
 (8 cups)
1 cup plain low-fat yogurt**

*Makes 6 servings
Preparation time: 20 minutes
plus 12 hours' setting time*

Mast

1. Bring the milk to a boil over medium heat in a very clean, nonreactive pot. Dirty or greasy utensils will not produce the desired results.

2. Remove the milk from heat and let stand until cool but not completely cold. The temperature of the milk is very important at this stage. It should not be too cold or too hot. If the milk is too cool, the culture will not grow; if it is too warm the heat will kill the bacteria in the culture. If you are using a thermometer, the temperature should be 115°F or 45°C, or with some experience you can test by hand. Put your little finger in the milk and count to 20. The temperature is correct if you can just tolerate the heat.

3. Pour the milk into a Pyrex dish, reserving 1 cup for step 4. Pull out the rack in the center shelf of the oven and place the dish on it.

4. Dilute the yogurt with 1 cup cooled milk. Gradually add this mixture to the four corners of the Pyrex dish. Cover the dish with its lid and gently push the rack back inside the oven. Close the oven door and turn on the inside light. **Do not heat the oven.** Allow to rest undisturbed at least overnight. (Yogurt must be stored in a draft-free, protected spot and not moved or touched during this period, and your oven is the ideal place for this. As an alternative, wrap the dish with a large towel or blanket and let it rest undisturbed in a corner of your kitchen for at least 24 hours.)

5. Keep the yogurt in the refrigerator and use as needed. *Nush-e Jan!*

Variation: Drained or thick yogurt (*mast-e kisei*): Pour the yogurt into 3 layers of cheesecloth or a cotton bag, pull the ends together and then hang the bag for 15 to 20 minutes over a large pot to catch the yogurt drips, or use a yogurt funnel. All the liquid will slowly drain out, leaving behind a thick and creamy yogurt.

Draining store-bought low-fat yogurt: Low-fat yogurt purchased in supermarkets can be drained and thickened by placing 3 or 4 layers of paper towel over the top of the bowl of yogurt for a few hours to absorb the excess liquid. Place the bowl of yogurt in a larger container to catch the drips from the paper towels and store the yogurt in the refrigerator. After a few hours remove the paper towel.

Yogurt and Spinach Dip

4 cups (10 ounces) fresh spinach, washed and chopped, or 1 cup frozen spinach
2 onions, peeled and thinly sliced
2 cloves garlic, peeled and crushed
2 tablespoons olive oil
1½ cups low-fat drained yogurt (page 11)

½ teaspoon salt
¼ teaspoon freshly ground black pepper
¼ teaspoon saffron dissolved in 1 tablespoon hot water
1 tablespoon rose petals

Makes 4 servings
Preparation time: 10 minutes
plus several hours' refrigeration
Cooking time: 45 minutes

Borani-e esfenaj

1. Steam the spinach in a steamer for 20 minutes or place the spinach in a pan, cover, and steam until wilted, about 5 minutes. Drain.

2. In a non-stick skillet, lightly brown the onions and garlic in 2 tablespoons oil for 20 minutes over medium heat.

3. Stir in the spinach and fry for 2 minutes. Remove from heat and let cool.

4. In a serving bowl, mix yogurt and spinach and season to taste with salt and pepper. Refrigerate for several hours before serving.

5. Garnish with saffron water and rose petals. Serve as an appetizer with Persian bread. *Nush-e Jan!*

Borani recipes are attributed to their namesake, the Sasanian queen Pourandokht. Queen Pourandokht was fond of yogurt, and her chef made her many dishes with drained yogurt and vegetables. These dishes were called Pourani after her, and in time Pourani became Borani.

Yogurt and Cucumber Dip with Rose Petals

Makes 4 servings
Preparation time: 15 minutes
plus 1 hour's refrigeration

هس خیار

Mast-o khiar

1 long seedless cucumber, peeled and diced
½ cup raisins, washed and drained
3 cups plain low-fat yogurt
¼ cup chopped scallions
1 tablespoon chopped fresh mint
2 tablespoons chopped fresh dill weed
2 tablespoons chopped fresh oregano
2 cloves garlic, peeled and crushed

3 tablespoons chopped shelled walnuts
1 teaspoon salt
¼ teaspoon freshly ground black pepper

Garnish
½ teaspoon chopped dried mint
3 tablespoons dried rose petals

1. In a serving bowl, combine cucumber, raisins, yogurt, scallions, mint, dill, oregano, garlic, and chopped walnuts. Mix thoroughly and season to taste with salt and pepper.

2. Refrigerate for at least 1 hour before serving.

3. Garnish with mint and rose petals. Serve with bread as an appetizer. *Nush-e Jan!*

Variation: In summer, this dip is frequently transformed into a refreshing cold soup by adding 1 cup of cold water and 2 or 3 ice cubes to the mixture.

Persian Cheese

½ gallon low-fat milk, 2% milk fat
1 cup plain low-fat yogurt
2 tablespoons salt (optional)
¼ cup fresh lime juice
Cheesecloth for straining
   the mixture
½ teaspoon salt for step 5

Makes 6 servings
Preparation and cooking time: 20
minutes plus 6 hours to settle
and set

Panir

1. Pour the milk into a large pot. Bring to a boil over low heat.

2. Add the yogurt, 2 tablespoons salt, and lime juice to the pot of milk. Mix well and simmer over low heat for 3 to 5 minutes, or until its color turns yellowish.

3. Line a strainer with three layers of cheesecloth and place the strainer in a large container. Remove the pot from the heat and immediately pour the milk-yogurt mixture over the cheesecloth. Let drain for several minutes. Save the liquid in the large container for step 5.

4. To remove excess water from the milk-yogurt mixture, bundle the free ends of cheesecloth together over the mixture to enclose it. Place the cheesecloth in the center of the strainer and place a heavy weight on top of the cheesecloth. Allow to stand for about 3 hours, then remove the weight and open up the cheesecloth. Remove the cheese and place it in a container. Refrigerate for 3 hours to set thoroughly.

5. Cut the cheese into pieces and place the pieces in a sterilized jar. Fill the jar with the strained liquid from step 3 and add ½ teaspoon salt. Refrigerate until ready to serve.

6. Serve the cheese with bread and fresh vegetables and herbs. *Nush-e Jan!*

Bread and Cheese with Fresh Vegetables and Herbs

 نان و پنیر و سبزی خوردن

Nan-o panir-o sabzi-khordan

No Persian table would be complete without *nan-o panir-o sabzi-khordan*, quite simply bread and fresh feta cheese with fresh greens, uncooked vegetables, herbs and nuts. *Nan-o panir-o sabzi-khordan* is eaten either as an appetizer or to accompany or conclude the main course. As an appetizer, small pieces of bread are spread with cheese and garnished with vegetables, herbs and nuts. With the main course, *sabzi-khordan* is passed around and a handful of the herbs and vegetables is selected by each individual according to taste. I consider small young fresh sprigs of basil, spring onions, and radishes to be essential ingredients of this mix. The ends should be cut off of the radishes, but some of the leaf should be left on; many people eat the radish leaf for its digestive properties. *Sabzi-khordan* can also include scallions, cilantro or coriander, watercress, tarragon, and mint.

Persian bread is called *nan*, and there are several kinds. *Nan-e-sangak,* or stone bread, is a large, flat, rectangular loaf, rounded on one end and about 3 feet long, 18 inches wide, and 1 inch thick. It is baked in the oven on hot stones and served warm. *Nan-e lavash* is a very thin, crisp bread in a round or oval shape. It keeps well for several days. *Nan-e barbari* is a flat, oval loaf, about 2 inches thick. It should be eaten very fresh and warm; it is usually served for breakfast.

Nan-e-sangak is available at Persian specialty stores. *Nan-e lavash* and *nan-e barbari* are available not only in specialty stores but often in your local supermarket.

Panir can be any of the cow's or goat's milk cheeses similar to feta cheese, or any soft, white cheese according to your taste.

Nush-e Jan!

Yogurt and Eggplant

2 large or 3 small seedless eggplants
1 tablespoon olive oil
1 large onion, peeled and thinly sliced
4 cloves garlic, peeled and crushed
1 teaspoon salt
¼ teaspoon freshly ground black pepper

1 cup low-fat drained yogurt (page 11) or whey (*kashk*)
1 tablespoon chopped fresh mint or 1 teaspoon dried
¼ teaspoon saffron dissolved in 1 tablespoon hot water
½ cup chopped walnuts (optional)

Makes 4 servings
Preparation time: 15 minutes
Cooking time: 1 hour

Borani-e bademjan

1. Preheat oven to 350°F.

2. Wash eggplants and prick in several places with a fork to prevent bursting. Place whole eggplants on oven rack and bake for 1 hour. Be sure to put a tray under the eggplant to catch drips.

3. Remove eggplants from oven, let cool, then peel and mash.

4. Heat the oil in a non-stick skillet and lightly brown the onion and garlic over medium heat. Add the eggplant and mix well. Cover and cook for five minutes over low heat. Add salt and pepper. Remove from heat and let cool.

5. Transfer to a serving dish, mix with yogurt or whey, and garnish with mint, saffron water, and walnuts.

6. Place the eggplant mixture on a platter. Cut up *lavash* bread and arrange around the platter. Serve as an appetizer. *Nush-e Jan!*

Variation: You may peel and cut the eggplants into thin lengthwise slices. Rinse with cold water, drain, and pat dry. Brush all sides with egg whites, then brown with 1 tablespoon oil in a non-stick pan over medium heat. Remove from the skillet and brown the onion and garlic. In a baking dish, layer the eggplant with the onion and garlic and whey diluted in ½ cup water. Garnish with mint, saffron and walnuts. Cover and bake for 15 minutes in a preheated 350°F oven. Uncover and bake 15 minutes longer.

Persian Chicken Salad

Makes 12 servings
Preparation time: 1 hour 30 minutes plus 2 hours' chilling time in refrigerator

سالادالیویه

Salad-e olivieh

1 frying chicken, about 2 or 3 pounds, with skin removed
1 onion, peeled and finely chopped
1 teaspoon salt
4 carrots, peeled and chopped
2 cups fresh shelled or frozen green peas
2 scallions, chopped
2 celery stalks, chopped
6 large potatoes, boiled, peeled, and chopped
3 medium cucumber pickles, finely chopped
½ cup chopped fresh parsley
⅔ cup green olives, pitted and chopped

3 hard-boiled eggs, peeled and chopped (optional)

Dressing
3 cups light mayonnaise
2 tablespoons Dijon mustard
2 tablespoons low-fat drained yogurt (page 11)
¼ cup olive oil
½ cup vinegar or lime juice
1½ teaspoons salt
½ teaspoon freshly ground black pepper

1. Place the chicken in a non-stick pot along with the onion and salt. Cover and cook for 1½ hours over low heat (no water is added because chicken makes its own juice). When done, allow to cool, debone the chicken, and chop finely.

2. Steam the carrots for 5 minutes and set aside.

3. Steam shelled peas for 5 minutes and set aside. (If using frozen peas, follow package directions.)

4. In a large bowl, whisk together mayonnaise, mustard, yogurt, olive oil, vinegar or lime juice, salt, and pepper. Mix thoroughly.

5. Combine chicken, prepared vegetables and eggs with the rest of the ingredients. Pour the dressing over it and toss well. Adjust seasoning to taste.

6. Transfer salad to a flat plate and decorate with hearts of romaine lettuce. Chill for at least 2 hours. Serve with hot pita, *lavash*, or French bread. *Nush-e Jan!*

Caviar

4 ounces Caspian Sea caviar
Thin toast
2 fresh limes, cut in half

Makes 4 servings

خاويار

Khaviar

Caviar is the unfertilized, processed roe of the sturgeon fish. Its name probably comes from the Persian *mahi-e khayehdar,* literally meaning egg-bearing fish. The best caviar comes from the Caspian Sea. There are three main types of caviar, each from a different species of sturgeon. The largest eggs, known by the Russian name beluga, come from the *fil-mahi,* literally elephant fish. The average-sized roe, osetra, comes from *tas-mahi,* or the bald fish; and the smallest eggs, sevruga, are those from the *uzun-brun,* or the long-nosed fish. Besides the size, each type has its own particular flavor, and you must try each to see which you prefer.

The most important step in the production of caviar is the salting. The different brands available vary in quality. As long as it comes from the Caspian Sea, it is the real thing, and then it is up to you to decide which type you prefer.

I have often been asked, "How does one know if caviar is fresh?" The best answer I can give is that it should smell of the sea but never fishy.

Around the Caspian there are various recipes that include the roe of the sturgeon. One is with garlic chives in an omelet (the Russians also like to garnish caviar with chopped onions and egg whites), but I believe good-quality caviar should be eaten simply. Place a good-sized dollop on a thin piece of lightly toasted bread and squeeze a little fresh lime juice over it. *Nush-e jan!*

Homemade Broth

Makes 6 cups
Preparation time: 20 minutes
Cooking time: 2 hours

Gusht abeh

1 teaspoon peppercorns
2 bay leaves
1 bunch dill (stalk and roots)
3 sprigs parsley
1 sprig coriander (stalk and roots)
4–5 pounds chicken parts (skinless drumsticks, breast bones, wings, backs, or scraps), or raw beef or veal bones

1 large onion, peeled and thinly sliced
2 cloves garlic, whole
2 carrots, chopped
2 celery stalks, chopped
2 leaks, chopped
1 parsnip, chopped
1 teaspoon salt

1. Bundle the peppercorns, bay leaves, dill, parsley, and coriander together, then place in a piece of cheesecloth and tie shut.

2. Place all the ingredients in a large pot. Cover with 8 cups water and bring to a boil. Skim off the froth as it rises.

3. Reduce heat, cover, and simmer for about 2 hours over low heat, adding more water if necessary.

4. Strain broth through a sieve and discard the solids. Allow broth to cool.

5. Pour broth into a gravy strainer (a container with a spout from the base that allows one to pour the liquid while the fat stays on top). Remove excess fat from the top, cover, and refrigerate. Use as needed. *Nush-e Jan!*

Note: Store-bought bouillon cubes will seem tame by comparison once you get used to the taste of homemade broth.

Lamb Shank Soup with Yellow Split Peas and Meat Paste

Makes 6 servings
Preparation time: 10 minutes
Cooking time: 2 hours 15 minutes

Abgusht-e lapeh-o gusht-e kubideh

2 pounds lamb shanks and 1 pound breast of lamb
2 large onions, peeled and quartered
6 cups water
1 cup yellow split peas
1 teaspoon turmeric
2 teaspoons salt
½ teaspoon freshly ground black pepper
3 large potatoes, peeled and cut into halves
4 tomatoes, peeled and sliced
1 tablespoon tomato paste

4 whole dried Persian limes (*limu-omani*), pierced, or ¼ cup lime juice
½ teaspoon ground saffron, dissolved in 2 tablespoons hot water
2 teaspoons ground cinnamon
½ teaspoon cumin
¼ teaspoon cardamom
¼ teaspoon rose petals

Garnish
1 large onion, peeled and sliced
1 teaspoon ground cinnamon

1. Place the meat in a large pot. Cover with cold water, bring to a boil, then drain and remove all the excess fat from the meat.

2. Place the meat, onion, and 6 cups of water in a large pot. Bring to a boil. Add split peas, turmeric, salt, and pepper. Cover and let simmer for 1½ hours over low heat.

3. Add the potatoes, tomatoes, tomato paste, pierced Persian limes or lime juice, saffron water, spices, and rose petals. Continue to simmer 45 minutes over low heat.

4. Test with a fork or knife tip to see if the meat and potatoes are tender. Adjust seasoning to taste.

5. Using a slotted spoon, remove all of the stew ingredients, leaving the broth in the pot. Debone the meat and reserve the bones. Mash the meat and vegetables together to make a paste called *gusht kubideh*. It should have the consistency of lumpy mashed potatoes. Iranian cooks would use a mortar and pestle to pound the *gusht kubideh* to just the right consistency. A food processor may be used instead, but take care not to let the paste get too smooth. Season to taste with salt and pepper and arrange on a serving platter.

6. Reheat the broth and scoop out the marrow from the bones. Mix the marrow with the broth, pour 3 tablespoons of the broth over the *gusht kubideh* and garnish with cinnamon and slices of new onion. Serve the remaining broth in a bowl as soup. Serve the *gusht kubideh* separately with Persian pickles (*torshi*), a platter of spring onions, radishes, fresh tarragon, basil, and mint (*sabzi-khordan*) and *lavash* or pita bread. *Nush-e Jan!*

Variation: This soup may also be made with beef or veal. You may substitute ¼ cup chickpeas and ¼ cup red kidney beans for the split peas.

Pomegranate Soup

Makes 6 servings
Preparation time: 20 minutes
Cooking time: 2 hours 5 minutes

آش انار

Ash-e anar

Notes: If you must use dried herbs, reduce the measurement to ¼ of the fresh herbs. Place the dried herbs in a sieve in a bowl of lukewarm water and allow to soak for 15 minutes. Remove the sieve and use the herbs as per the recipe.

Gol-par means angelica seeds, which comes literally from the Persian compound word *gol* (flower) and *pari* (angel).

4 onions, 3 peeled and thinly sliced, 1 peeled and grated
3 cloves garlic, peeled and crushed
3 tablespoons olive oil
½ cup yellow split peas
8 cups water
1¼ teaspoons salt
½ teaspoon freshly ground black pepper
1 teaspoon turmeric
2 cups and 2 tablespoons chopped fresh parsley
2 cups chopped fresh coriander leaves
1 cup chopped fresh mint
2 cups chopped fresh chives or scallions
1 beet, peeled and chopped

½ pound lean ground beef, veal or lamb
1 cup rice
⅔ cup pomegranate paste diluted in 2 cups of water, or 4 cups pomegranate juice, or 4 cups fresh pomegranate seeds
⅓ cup sugar
2 tablespoons angelica powder (*gol-par*)

Garnish
1 tablespoon olive oil
5 cloves garlic, peeled and crushed
2 tablespoons dried mint flakes
½ teaspoon turmeric
2 tablespoons pomegranate seeds
1 tablespoon angelica seeds

1. In a large, heavy non-stick pot, lightly brown the 3 sliced onions and garlic with 2 tablespoons olive oil over medium heat for 20 minutes. Add split peas and continue to sauté for a few minutes longer. Add 8 cups water. Bring to boil, reduce heat, partially cover, and simmer over medium heat for 20 minutes.

2. Add 1 teaspoon salt, ¼ teaspoon pepper, turmeric, 2 cups parsley, coriander, mint, chives or scallions, and beet. Continue cooking for 20 minutes longer, stirring occasionally with a wooden spoon to prevent sticking.

3. Combine the grated onion and the meat in a bowl. Season with ¼ teaspoon salt, ¼ teaspoon pepper and 2 tablespoons chopped parsley. Mix ingredients thoroughly, shape into chestnut-size meatballs and add them to the pot.

4. Add rice, partially cover and cook for 30 minutes longer.

5. Stir in diluted pomegranate paste, sugar, and angelica powder, and simmer over low heat for 35 minutes.

6. Check a meatball to see if it is cooked and taste soup for seasoning. It should be sweet and sour. Add warm water if the soup is too thick.

7. Just before serving, heat 1 tablespoon of oil in a non-stick skillet and brown the garlic. Remove from heat. Crumble the dried mint flakes in the palm of your hand and add to the garlic. Add ½ teaspoon turmeric; mix well.

8. Pour the warmed soup into a tureen and garnish with the mint-and-garlic mixture, pomegranate seeds, and angelica seeds. *Nush-e Jan!*

For best results, make your *ash* a day in advance to give the flavors a chance to meld; reheat it just before serving. Add the garnish at the last minute, after pouring the soup into the tureen.

Cream of Barley

Makes 6 servings
Preparation time: 20 minutes
Cooking time: 1 hour 45 minutes

2 onions, peeled and thinly sliced
2 cloves garlic, peeled and crushed
1 tablespoon olive oil
4 cups water
½ cup barley
1 teaspoon salt
¼ teaspoon freshly ground
    black pepper
3 cups homemade beef or
    chicken broth (page 27)

1 carrot, peeled and grated
3 leeks, finely chopped
½ cup light sour cream
Juice of 1 lime

Garnish
2 tablespoons chopped fresh parsley
Zest of ½ lime, minced (optional)

Soup-e jow

1. In a large non-stick pot, lightly brown onions and garlic in 1 tablespoon oil over medium heat, then add the water, barley, salt, and pepper. Bring to a boil. Cover, reduce heat, and simmer for 1 hour or until barley is tender, stirring occasionally.

2. Add the broth, carrot, and leeks to the soup. Cover and simmer over low heat for 30 to 40 minutes longer. Using a slotted spoon, remove ingredients and place in a blender; add sour cream and lime juice and correct seasoning to taste, adding more salt, pepper or lime juice. Blend thoroughly and return to the pot. If the soup is too thick, add more warm water. Continue cooking for another five minutes.

3. Just before serving, garnish the soup with parsley and the lime zest. *Nush-e Jan!*

Mung Bean Soup

Makes 6 servings
Preparation time: 20 minutes
Cooking time: 3 hours

Ash-e mash

Notes: If you must use dried herbs, reduce the measurement to ¼ of the fresh herbs. Place the dried herbs in a sieve in a bowl of lukewarm water and allow to soak for 15 minutes. Remove the sieve and use the herbs as per the recipe.

Mung beans are tiny gray-green beans that are usually forced to germinate for bean sprouts. They are available in specialty stores.

2 large onions, peeled and thinly sliced
5 cloves garlic, peeled and crushed
1 tablespoon olive oil
2 teaspoons salt
¼ teaspoon freshly ground black pepper
1 teaspoon turmeric
1 cup dried mung beans
10 cups water
½ cup rice
1 cup diced turnip
1 cup peeled and diced fresh pumpkin or other winter squash
1 cup chopped fresh coriander leaves

2 cups chopped fresh parsley
½ cup chopped fresh dill
1 cup chopped fresh chives or scallions
1 cup pearl onions, peeled (optional)
3 cups defatted chicken broth
1 cup liquid whey or light sour cream

Garnish
5 cloves garlic, peeled and crushed
1 tablespoon olive oil
1 tablespoon dried mint flakes
1 teaspoon turmeric

1. In a large non-stick pot, lightly brown the onions and garlic in 1 tablespoon oil over medium heat. Add salt, pepper, and turmeric. Add mung beans. Sauté for a few minutes. Pour in the water and bring to a boil, skimming the froth as it forms. Reduce heat, cover, and simmer for 50 minutes over medium heat, stirring occasionally with a wooden spoon.

2. Add the rice, turnip, pumpkin, coriander, parsley, dill, chives, pearl onions, and the chicken broth. Cover partially and simmer gently for another 1½ hours, stirring occasionally.

3. Check to see if beans and vegetables are done. If desired, using a slotted spoon, remove some of the ingredients and place in a blender; blend thoroughly and return to the pot. Add whey or sour cream; mix well and adjust seasoning.

4. Meanwhile, prepare the garnish. Brown the garlic in a non-stick skillet with 1 tablespoon oil and remove from heat. Crumble the dried mint flakes in your hand and add to the garlic. Add the turmeric and mix well.

5. Pour soup into a tureen. Decorate the soup with the garnish. Stir the garnish in just before ladling soup into individual bowls. *Nush-e Jan!*

For best results, make your *ash* a day in advance to give the flavors a chance to meld; reheat it just before serving. Add the garnish, warmed, at the last minute, after pouring the soup into the tureen.

Variation: Peel and slice 3 eggplants. Fry on both sides in 2 tablespoons oil, and add in step 3.

Sweet and Sour Soup

Makes 6 servings
Preparation time: 30 minutes
Cooking time: 2 hours 30 minutes

آش ميوه

Ash-e miveh

Note: If you must use dried herbs, reduce the measurement to ¼ the fresh herbs. Place the dried herbs in a sieve in a bowl of lukewarm water and allow to soak for 15 minutes. Remove the sieve and use the herbs as per the recipe.

3 onions, 2 peeled and thinly sliced, 1 peeled and grated
1 pound lean ground meat or chicken
1 teaspoon salt
½ teaspoon freshly ground black pepper
½ teaspoon ground cinnamon
1 cup and 2 tablespoons chopped fresh parsley
1 tablespoon olive oil
½ teaspoon turmeric
½ cup dried yellow split peas or chickpeas
8–10 cups water
½ cup chopped fresh chives or scallions
½ cup chopped fresh beet leaves

¼ cup chopped fresh mint
1 cup chopped fresh coriander leaves
1 cup dried pitted prunes
1 cup dried apricots
½ cup rice
¼ cup chopped walnuts
¼ cup sugar
¼ cup red wine vinegar

Garnish
1 large onion, peeled and finely sliced
5 cloves garlic, peeled and crushed
1 tablespoon olive oil
1 tablespoon dried mint flakes, crushed
¼ teaspoon turmeric

1. In a mixing bowl, combine grated onion with ground meat. Add ½ teaspoon salt, ¼ teaspoon pepper, ¼ teaspoon cinnamon, and 2 tablespoons parsley. Mix well and shape into meatballs the size of walnuts.

2. In a large non-stick pot, brown the 2 sliced onions in 1 tablespoon oil over medium heat. Sprinkle with ¼ teaspoon salt, ¼ teaspoon pepper, ¼ teaspoon cinnamon and ½ teaspoon turmeric. Add the split peas or chickpeas, sauté for a few more minutes and pour in 8 cups water. Bring to a boil, reduce heat, cover, and simmer for 25 minutes over medium heat, stirring occasionally with a wooden spoon.

3. Add 1 cup parsley, chives or scallions, beet leaves, fresh mint, and coriander and simmer, covered, 25 minutes longer.

4. Add prunes, apricots, and meatballs; cover and simmer 25 minutes more.

5. Add rice and walnuts; cover and cook for 45 minutes longer.

6. Mix the sugar and vinegar together and stir into the soup. Cook for about 25 minutes longer. Add more warm water if *ash* is too thick. Taste for seasoning and add more sugar or vinegar if needed to balance the sweet and sour.

7. Shortly before serving, prepare the garnish by browning the onion and garlic in 1 tablespoon oil in a non-stick frying pan. Remove from heat; add crushed mint flakes and turmeric to the pan and mix well.

8. Pour warmed soup into a tureen. Pour the garlic-and-mint garnish on top and serve with Persian flat bread, *sangak* or *lavash. Nush-e Jan!*

Note: For richer, more developed flavors, make your *ash* the night before. Just before serving, warm up the soup and add the garnish mixture of browned onions, garlic, and mint.

Noodle Soup

Makes 6 servings
Preparation time: 20 minutes
Cooking time: 3 hours 30 minutes

Ash-e reshteh

Notes: Noodles are often served on Nowruz, the Iranian New Year's Day. Another traditional occasion is on the third day after friends and relatives have gone away on a trip. It is believed that by eating noodles we can send the travelers luck as they follow the path of their journey.

If you must use dried herbs, reduce the measurement to ¼ of the fresh herbs. Place the dried herbs in a sieve in a bowl of lukewarm water and allow to soak for 15 minutes. Remove the sieve and use the herbs as per the recipe.

3 large onions, peeled and thinly sliced
5 cloves garlic, peeled and crushed
2 tablespoons olive oil
2 teaspoons salt
½ teaspoon freshly ground black pepper
1 teaspoon turmeric
¼ cup dried red kidney beans, washed and soaked in cold water for 2 hours and drained
¼ cup dried navy beans
¼ cup dried chickpeas
10–12 cups water
½ cup lentils
2 cups homemade defatted beef broth (page 27)
½ cup coarsely chopped fresh chives or scallions
½ cup chopped fresh dill
1 cup coarsely chopped fresh parsley

6 cups spinach, washed and chopped, or 3 cups frozen spinach, chopped
1 fresh beet, peeled and diced in ½-inch pieces
½ pound Persian noodles (*reshteh*) or linguine noodles, broken in half
1 tablespoon all-purpose flour
1 cup liquid whey (*kashk*), or light sour cream, or ¼ cup wine vinegar

Garnish
1 onion, peeled and finely sliced
6 cloves of garlic, peeled and crushed
1 tablespoon olive oil
1 teaspoon turmeric
2 tablespoons dried mint flakes, crushed

1. In a large non-stick pot, brown the 3 onions and garlic in 2 tablespoons olive oil over medium heat. Add salt, pepper, and turmeric. Add kidney beans, navy beans, and chickpeas; sauté for a few minutes. Pour in 10 cups water and bring to boil, skim the froth as it forms, reduce heat, cover, and simmer for 45 minutes over medium heat.

2. Add lentils and beef broth. Cook 55 minutes longer.

3. Add chopped chives or scallions, dill, parsley, spinach, and the beet. Continue cooking, stirring from time to time for 1½ hours or until the beans are tender. Add salt and pepper to taste, and add more water if the *ash* is too thick.

4. Add noodles and flour and cook about 10 minutes, stirring occasionally.

5. Stir in the whey (or sour cream or vinegar), saving a dollop for the garnish, and mix well with a wooden spoon.

6. To prepare the garnish, brown the onion and garlic in oil in a non-stick frying pan. Remove from heat; add the turmeric and the crushed mint flakes and mix well.

7. Pour the soup into a tureen. Garnish with mint mixture and the dollop of whey. *Nush-e Jan!*

Pistachio Soup

1 cup pistachios, shelled
1 tablespoon olive oil
1 shallot, chopped
1 leek, chopped
1 clove garlic, peeled and chopped
2 tablespoons rice flour
6 cups homemade defatted chicken
    broth (page 27)

1 teaspoon salt
¼ teaspoon pepper
½ cup Seville orange juice or a mix-
    ture of 2 tablespoons fresh lime
    juice and ¼ cup fresh orange
    juice
2 tablespoons slivered pistachios for
    garnish

Makes 4 servings
Preparation time: 10 minutes
Cooking time: 55 minutes

Soup-e pesteh

1. Grind pistachios in a food processor or grinder.

2. In a heavy non-stick pot, heat oil over medium heat. Add shallot, leek, and garlic. Cover and gently stew until translucent. Add rice flour, stirring constantly with a wooden spoon. Add chicken broth and bring to a boil.

3. Add pistachios, salt, and pepper and reduce heat. Cover and simmer over low heat for 45 minutes, stirring occasionally.

4. Add Seville orange juice. Adjust seasoning.

5. Pour the soup into a tureen, garnish with slivered pistachios, and serve hot or cold. *Nush-e Jan!*

Variation: Pistachios can be substituted with almonds or hazelnuts.

Stuffed Grape Leaves

Makes 6 to 8 servings
Preparation time: 1 hour
Cooking time: 2 hours 25 minutes

Dolmeh-ye barg-e mo

Note: If you must use dried herbs, reduce the measurement to ¼ of the fresh herbs. Place the dried herbs in a sieve in a bowl of lukewarm water and allow to soak for 15 minutes. Remove the sieve and use the herbs as per the recipe.

50 fresh grape leaves in season or canned leaves
⅔ cup rice
¼ cup yellow split peas
1 teaspoon salt
1 onion, peeled and thinly sliced
½ pound lean ground meat (lamb, veal, or beef)
1 cup chopped scallions
¼ cup summer savory
½ cup chopped fresh dill
¼ cup chopped fresh tarragon
¼ cup chopped fresh mint
2½ cups chopped fresh parsley
Juice of 1 lime
¼ teaspoon freshly ground black pepper
1 teaspoon ground cinnamon
2 cups defatted broth (page 27)
2 tablespoons olive oil
⅔ cup sugar
⅓ cup vinegar
⅓ cup fresh lime juice

1. If using fresh grape leaves, pick small and tender ones, blanch them in boiling water for 2 minutes, then drain in a colander and rinse with cold water. For canned grape leaves, drain in a colander and rinse under cold running water.

2. In a saucepan, cook rice and split peas for 20 minutes over medium heat in 3 cups of water and ½ teaspoon salt. Drain in a colander.

3. In a non-stick skillet, brown onion and meat over medium heat for 20 minutes. Add the rice and split peas, scallions, summer savory, dill, tarragon, mint, parsley, and the juice of 1 lime. Season with ½ teaspoon salt, ¼ teaspoon pepper, and cinnamon. Mix this stuffing thoroughly, using hands or a wooden spoon.

4. Preheat oven to 350°F.

5. Place three layers of grape leaves on the bottom of an ovenproof dish oiled with 2 tablespoons olive oil.

6. Place a grape leaf on top of a wooden board with the vein side up and nip off the little stem. Top with 1 tablespoon stuffing. Roll up the leaf, folding in the ends to prevent the stuffing from leaking out while cooking. Arrange the stuffed grape leaves side by side in the dish.

7. Pour broth into the dish. Place a small ovenproof plate on top of the stuffed grape leaves to keep them down. Cover and bake in the oven for 1 hour.

8. Mix the sugar, vinegar, and lime juice. Remove the baking dish from oven, uncover the grape leaves, and baste with this syrup. Cover and return to oven. Bake for 45 minutes to 1 hour longer.

9. When the grape leaves are tender, taste sauce and adjust seasoning. The sauce should be quite reduced. Serve in the same baking dish or on a platter, while hot or warm, with bread and yogurt, or cool as an appetizer. *Nush-e Jan!*

Variation: Stuffed Grape Leaves with Pine Nuts (*Dolmeh-ye barg-e mo ba senobar*)—You may replace the meat with ⅓ cup pine nuts.

Stuffed Cabbage Leaves

Makes 6 servings
Preparation time: 30 minutes
Cooking time: 2 hours 35 minutes

Dolmeh-ye kalam

2 large heads of green or savory cabbage
¼ cup rice
¼ cup yellow split peas
1 onion, peeled and thinly sliced
1 pound lean ground meat (lamb, veal or beef)
2 tablespoons non-preservative tomato paste
¼ cup chopped fresh parsley
2 tablespoons chopped fresh mint
2 tablespoons chopped fresh dill
1 tablespoon chopped fresh tarragon

1 teaspoon salt
¼ teaspoon freshly ground black pepper
1 teaspoon ground cumin
½ teaspoon ground cinnamon
1½ cups fresh squeezed tomato juice
2 tablespoons olive oil
½ cup brown sugar
⅓ cup vinegar or ½ cup fresh lime juice

1. Core cabbage and remove individual leaves. Plunge them into boiling salted water. Cover and boil for 5 minutes, drain in colander, and rinse under cold water.

2. Cook rice and split peas in 2½ cups water and ½ teaspoon salt for 30 minutes. Drain.

3. In a non-stick skillet, brown onion and meat over medium heat for 20 minutes. Add tomato paste and mix thoroughly.

4. Combine meat, rice, split peas, and chopped herbs in a large bowl. Season with salt, pepper, cumin, and cinnamon. Mix well.

5. Preheat the oven to 350°F.

6. Place two layers of cabbage leaves in an ovenproof dish.

7. Place each leaf on a plate. Top with 1 tablespoon of stuffing. Roll tightly, folding in the sides of the leaf to prevent the stuffing from leaking out while cooking. Arrange stuffed cabbage leaves side by side in the dish.

8. Pour the tomato juice and 2 tablespoons oil into the dish around the stuffed leaves. Cover and bake in the oven for 1½ hours.

9. Combine brown sugar and vinegar or lime juice. Pour this mixture into the baking dish. Cover, return to oven, and bake 30 minutes more. Baste the stuffed cabbage leaves occasionally with pan juices.

10. When the stuffed cabbage leaves are done, taste sauce and adjust seasoning by adding more vinegar or sugar. Serve hot or warm in same baking dish with bread and yogurt on the side, or cool as an appetizer. *Nush-e Jan!*

Note: If you must use dried herbs, reduce the measurement to ¼ of the fresh herbs. Place the dried herbs in a sieve in a bowl of lukewarm water and allow to soak for 15 minutes. Remove the sieve and use the herbs as per the recipe.

Stuffed Quince

6 medium quince, similar in size
½ cup brown sugar
1 onion, peeled and thinly sliced
½ pound lean ground meat
¼ cup rice
1 teaspoon salt
¼ teaspoon freshly ground
   black pepper
1 teaspoon cinnamon

½ teaspoon cardamom
½ teaspoon cumin
1 teaspoon dried rose petals
1 cup apple juice
2 tablespoons olive oil
¼ cup balsamic vinegar
¼ cup lime juice
¼ teaspoon saffron, dissolved in
   1 tablespoon hot water

Makes 6 servings
Preparation time: 45 minutes
Cooking time: 1 hour 30 minutes

Dolmeh-ye beh

1. Wash and rub quince to remove fuzz. Cut off tops and set aside. Hollow out quince, using the tip of a knife or a melon baller to scoop out the seeds and some of the pulp, leaving a shell about ½ inch thick and reserving pulp. Sprinkle 1 teaspoon brown sugar in each quince shell.

2. In a non-stick skillet, fry onion and meat over medium heat for 15 minutes. Add rice, ½ cup water, 1 teaspoon salt, pepper, cinnamon, cardamom, cumin and rose petals. Bring to a boil. Cover and simmer for 15 minutes over low heat; remove from heat and mix thoroughly.

3. Fill each quince with stuffing, replace tops, and arrange side by side in a deep lidded pan. Add apple juice and the quince pulp to the pan and pour 2 tablespoons oil over the quince. Place 2 layers of paper towel over the pan and cover tightly with the lid. Simmer over low heat for 1 hour.

4. In a saucepan, combine vinegar, lime juice, remaining brown sugar, and saffron water. Pour over the fruit in the pan. Cover and cook for 45 minutes to one hour, basting occasionally with pan juices.

5. Check to see if fruit is tender and adjust seasonings to taste with sugar or vinegar. Serve in same dish or on a platter. Serve with bread, yogurt, and fresh herbs. *Nush-e Jan!*

Variation: Stuffed Apples (*Dolmeh-ye sib*)—You can replace the quince with baking apples. Cover and bake apples in a 350°F preheated oven for 30 minutes. Remove from the oven, add mixture from step 4, return to oven and bake for another 30 minutes uncovered.

Eggplant Casserole

3 large unpeeled eggplants, chopped in cubes
1 large green or yellow pepper, chopped
2 large onions, peeled and chopped
2 stalks celery, chopped
4 large tomatoes, peeled and chopped

1 whole garlic bulb, peeled and crushed
½ cup olive oil
3 teaspoons salt
1 teaspoon freshly ground black pepper
3 bay leaves
3 sprigs of thyme

Makes 6 servings
Preparation time: 20 minutes
Cooking time: 1 hour

یتیمچه بادمجان

Yatim-cheh bademjan

1. Preheat oven to 500°F.

2. Place all the vegetables in a large baking dish.

3. In a bowl, combine olive oil, salt, pepper, bay leaves and thyme and pour this mixture over the vegetables, mixing gently but thoroughly.

4. Bake uncovered on middle rack of oven for 30 minutes. Open the oven, pull out the rack and mix the vegetables gently. Push back the rack and continue baking for another 30 minutes.

5. Serve hot or cold. *Nush-e Jan!*

Eggplant Kuku

2 large eggplants, about 2 pounds
1 egg white
4 tablespoons olive oil
2 large onions, peeled and thinly
   sliced
2 cloves garlic, peeled and crushed
4 eggs
1 tablespoon chopped parsley
   (optional)

¼ teaspoon ground saffron, dissolved in 1 tablespoon hot water
4 tablespoons fresh lime juice
1 teaspoon baking powder
1 tablespoon all-purpose flour
1 teaspoon salt
¼ teaspoon freshly ground
   black pepper

Makes 4 servings
Preparation time: 35 minutes
Cooking time: 1 hour 40 minutes

Kuku-ye bademjan

1. To remove bitterness from the eggplants, peel them and cut each into 5 length-wise slices. Soak in a large bowl of water with 2 tablespoons salt for 20 minutes, then drain. Rinse with cold water and pat dry. Brush all sides of the eggplant with egg white.

2. In a non-stick skillet, brown eggplant on both sides in 1 tablespoon oil. Remove from the skillet, cool, and mash with a fork.

3. In the same skillet, lightly brown onion and garlic in 1 tablespoon oil over medium heat for 20 minutes; add to mashed eggplant.

4. Preheat oven to 350°F.

5. Break eggs into a bowl. Add parsley, saffron water, lime juice, baking powder, flour, salt, and pepper. Beat thoroughly with a fork. Add the eggplant mixture to beaten eggs. Mix thoroughly. Adjust seasoning to taste.

6. Pour 1 tablespoon oil into an 8-inch non-stick ovenproof baking dish and place it in the oven. Heat the oil; pour in the egg mixture and bake uncovered for 30 minutes. Remove the dish and gently pour 1 tablespoon oil over the egg mixture. Put the dish back in the oven and bake for 20 to 30 minutes longer, until golden brown.

7. Serve *kuku* in the baking dish or unmold it by loosening the edge with knife and inverting it onto a serving platter. *Nush-e Jan!*

Variation 1: *Kuku* can also be cooked on top of the stove. Heat 2 tablespoons oil in a non-stick skillet, pour in the egg mixture, then cook, covered, over low heat until it has set, about 25 to 30 minutes. Cook the second side by cutting the *kuku* into wedges and turning them over one by one; add the rest of the oil, cover, and cook for 15 to 20 minutes longer, or until golden brown.

Variation 2: You may also use an extra-large non-stick muffin pan to bake individual *kuku*s. Pour one teaspoon of oil into each muffin cup, heat the oil, pour in the eggplant mixture, and place in a 350°F oven for 30 minutes. Remove from the oven and pour another teaspoon of oil over the *kuku*s. Return to the oven and bake for 15 minutes longer.

Fresh Herb Kuku

Makes 4 servings
Preparation time: 25 minutes
Cooking time: 1 hour

کوکوی سبزی

Kuku-ye sabzi

Note: If you must use dried herbs, reduce the measurement to ¼ of the fresh herbs. Place the dried herbs in a sieve in a bowl of lukewarm water and allow to soak for 15 minutes. Remove the sieve and use the herbs as per the recipe.

5 eggs
1 teaspoon baking powder
¼ stick cinnamon
¼ teaspoon cardamom
¼ teaspoon cumin
¼ teaspoon rose petals
1 teaspoon salt
¼ teaspoon freshly ground
black pepper
2 cloves garlic, peeled and crushed
1 cup finely chopped fresh chives or
scallions

1 cup finely chopped fresh parsley
leaves
1 cup finely chopped fresh coriander
leaves
1 cup chopped fresh dill
1 tablespoon dried fenugreek
(optional)
2 tablespoons dried barberries
(optional)
4 tablespoons olive oil
1 tablespoon all-purpose flour

Herb kuku is a traditional New Year's dish in Iran. The green of the herbs symbolizes rebirth. Eggs represent fertility and happiness for the year to come.

1. Preheat oven to 350°F.

2. Break eggs into a large bowl. Add baking powder, cinnamon, cardamom, cumin, rose petals, salt and pepper. Beat with a fork. Add garlic, chopped herbs, fenugreek, barberries, 1 tablespoon oil, and flour and mix thoroughly. Adjust seasoning to your taste.

3. Pour 2 tablespoons of the olive oil into a non-stick 8-inch ovenproof baking dish; place it in the oven for 5 minutes to heat the oil. Pour in the egg mixture and bake uncovered for 30 minutes. Remove the dish and gently pour the remaining oil over the *kuku*. Return the dish to the oven and bake for 20 to 30 minutes longer, until golden brown.

4. Serve *kuku* in the baking dish or unmold it by loosening the edge with a knife and inverting it onto a serving platter. Cut the *kuku* into small pieces and serve hot or cold with *lavash* bread and yogurt. *Nush-e Jan!*

Variation 1: *Kuku* can also be cooked on top of the stove. Heat the oil or butter in a non-stick skillet, pour in the egg mixture, then cook, covered, over low heat until it has set, about 25 to 30 minutes. Cook the second side by cutting the kuku into wedges and turning them over one by one; add more oil or butter if needed. Cover and cook for 20 to 30 minutes longer, or until golden brown.

Variation 2: You may also use an extra-large non-stick muffin pan to bake individual *kukus*. Pour one teaspoon of oil into each muffin cup, heat the oil, pour in the eggplant mixture, and place in a 350°F oven for 30 minutes. Remove from the oven and pour another teaspoon of oil on the top of the *kukus*. Return to the oven and bake 15 minutes longer.

Tenderloin Kabab

Makes 4 servings
Preparation time: 20 minutes
plus 24 hours' marinating
Cooking time: 10 minutes

کباب برگ

Kabab-e barg

2 pounds lean boned tenderloin or
    sirloin (lamb, beef or veal)
1 large onion, peeled and sliced
4 cloves garlic, peeled and crushed
½ teaspoon freshly ground black
    pepper
¾ cup fresh lime juice
2 teaspoons salt
¼ teaspoon ground saffron, dis-
    solved in 1 tablespoon hot water
1 cup low-fat yogurt

8 cherry tomatoes or 4 large toma-
    toes, cut in quarters

For Basting:
2 tablespoons olive oil
Juice of 2 limes
1 teaspoon salt

1 12-ounce package of *lavash* bread
2 tablespoons sumac powder
    (optional)

1. Have your butcher remove the backbone from the lamb loins; remove the fillets from the loins, and trim all fat and gristle from the main muscle. Cut meat lengthwise into 3-by-4-by-¼-inch pieces. Pound each piece with a mallet or heavy knife blade and place meat in a large stainless steel or Pyrex pot.

2. Add onion, garlic, pepper, lime juice, salt, saffron water and yogurt to the pot. Mix well. Cover the meat and marinate for at least 24 hours in refrigerator. Turn the meat in the marinade twice during this period.

3. Start a bed of charcoal at least 30 minutes before you want to cook and let it burn until the coals glow. (You may use a hair dryer to speed up this process.)

4. During this time, thread each piece of meat onto a flat, sword-like skewer, leaving a few inches free on both ends. Spear tomatoes on separate skewers.

5. For basting, combine oil, the juice of 2 limes, and 1 teaspoon salt in a small saucepan. Keep warm.

6. When coals are ready, brush the tomatoes and meat lightly with the baste. Place tomatoes on the grill first, then place the skewered meat on the grill. Cook for 3 or 4 minutes on each side, turning the skewers constantly. The meat should be seared on the outside, pink and juicy on the inside.

7. Spread *lavash* bread on a serving platter. When the meat is cooked, place the skewers of meat on the bread and brush them with the lime and saffron mixture. Garnish with grilled tomatoes. Sprinkle the kababs with sumac powder. Try it to taste. Cover with lavash bread to keep the food warm.

8. Serve immediately with *chelow* (saffron steamed rice, page 88), *lavash* bread, *torshi* (Persian pickles) and a dish of fresh herbs, especially scallions and basil. Remove the meat from each skewer by placing a piece of *lavash* bread over several pieces of meat and using it to hold down the meat while you pull it off the skewer. *Nush-e Jan!*

Variation: Lamb Rib Chops Kabab (*Shish lik*) may be substituted for loins.

Shish Kabab

Makes 4 servings
Preparation time: 30 minutes
plus 24 hours' marinating
Cooking time: 10 minutes

Shish kabab

2 pounds lamb, veal, or beef, from the boned loin or leg, or boneless chicken breast, cut into 2-inch cubes
4 green peppers, with seeds and ribs removed, cut into 2-inch squares
6 large tomatoes, quartered
10 cloves garlic, peeled
10 pearl onions or 3 large ones peeled and cut into 2-inch cubes

10 mushrooms
1 large onion, peeled and grated
⅔ cup vinegar
½ cup olive oil
1 teaspoon salt
1 teaspoon dried oregano

1 12 ounce package of *lavash* bread

1. Pound each piece of meat with a small mallet. Spear meat cubes onto wooden skewers, alternating them with pieces of pepper, tomato, garlic, onions, and mushrooms. Place finished skewers in a large flat laminated pan.

2. In a large bowl, combine grated onion, vinegar, olive oil, salt and oregano. Mix well. Pour over the shish kababs, cover, and marinate for at least 24 hours in a refrigerator.

3. Start a bed of charcoal at least 30 minutes before you want to cook and let it burn until the coals are glowing. (You may use a hair dryer to speed up this process.)

4. When coals are evenly lit with white ash around each coal and the grill is hot, place meat on grill rack. Grill for 3 to 5 minutes on each side.

5. Spread whole *lavash* bread on a serving platter. Arrange the skewers on the bread, cover with another piece of *lavash* to keep the shish kababs warm, and serve immediately with scallions, basil, and yogurt. *Nush-e Jan!*

Variation: As an alternative, you may marinate with 1 cup of low-fat yogurt, 1 grated onion, 2 tablespoons fresh lime juice, ½ teaspoon ground saffron dissolved in 2 tablespoons hot water, and ⅓ teaspoon freshly ground black pepper.

Chicken Kabab

Makes 4 servings
Preparation time: 20 minutes
plus 6 hours' marinating
Cooking time: 15 minutes

Jujeh kabab

Note: You may also broil the chicken pieces in a pan (without using skewers) in a broiler for 10 minutes on each side. When cooking, the door of the broiler should be shut to ensure that the broiled chicken will be tender.

1 teaspoon ground saffron, dissolved in 2 tablespoons hot water
1 cup fresh lime juice
2 tablespoons olive oil
2 large onions, peeled and thinly sliced
1 teaspoon salt
2 broiling chickens, about 4 pounds, each cut into 10 pieces, or 4 pounds of chicken drumettes, with skin and all excess fat removed (chicken drumettes are tastier and cheaper)
10 cherry tomatoes or 4 large tomatoes, cut into quarters

For Basting:
Juice of 1 lime
2 tablespoons olive oil or butter
1 teaspoon salt
1 teaspoon freshly ground black pepper

Garnish
Limes
Parsley sprigs

2 12-ounce packages of *lavash* bread

1. In a large bowl, combine 1 teaspoon saffron water, lime juice, olive oil, onions, and salt. Beat well with a fork. Add the pieces of chicken and toss well with marinade. Cover and marinate for at least 6 hours and up to 2 days in the refrigerator.

2. Start a bed of charcoal at least 30 minutes before you want to cook and let it burn until the coals glow evenly. (You may use a hair dryer to speed up the process.) Otherwise, preheat the oven broiler.

3. Skewer the tomatoes on the skewers.

4. Spear wings, breasts, and legs on different skewers (they require different cooking times).

5. For basting, combine the juice of 1 lime with the remaining saffron water, 2 tablespoons olive oil, 1 teaspoon salt, and 1 teaspoon pepper. Mix well and set aside.

6. Grill the chicken and tomatoes 8 to 15 minutes (drumettes need less time to cook), putting the legs on first, then the breasts and wings. Turn occasionally. The chicken is done when the juice that runs out is yellow rather than pink.

7. Spread a whole *lavash* bread on a serving platter. Paint the chicken with the baste mixture. Remove the grilled chicken from skewers and arrange the pieces on the bread. Garnish with limes cut in half and sprigs of parsley. Cover the platter with more bread to keep the kababs warm.

8. Serve immediately with fresh herbs, *torshi* (Persian pickles), and french fries. *Nush-e Jan!*

Chicken Stuffed with Rice

Makes 4 servings
Preparation time: 35 minutes
Cooking time: 1 hour 55 minutes

Morgh-e tu por ba berenj

Note: Clean sand from barberries (*zereshk*) by removing their stems and placing barberries in a colander. Place colander in a large container full of cold water and allow barberries to soak for 20 minutes. The sand will settle to the bottom of the container. Take the colander out of the container and run cold water over the barberries; set aside.

2 small frying chickens, about 6 to 7 pounds, or 2 Cornish game hens
2 teaspoons salt
2 large onions, peeled and thinly sliced
2 cloves garlic, peeled and crushed
1 tablespoon olive oil
½ cup rice, cleaned and washed
¼ teaspoon cumin
¼ teaspoon cardamom
¼ teaspoon cinnamon
1 teaspoon dried rose petals
¼ teaspoon freshly ground black pepper
1 cup homemade defatted chicken broth (page 27)
¼ cup dried barberries, cleaned, soaked for 20 minutes, and drained
2 tablespoons slivered almonds
2 tablespoons raisins
2 tablespoons fresh lime juice
¼ teaspoon ground saffron, dissolved in 1 tablespoon hot water
¼ cup apple juice
Lime slices for garnish

This stuffing can also be used for turkey with good results.

1. Clean and wash chickens or hens. Remove the skin and trim all the excess fat from the chicken. Open the cavity and pull out the excess fat. Rub chickens or hens with 1 teaspoon salt.

2. In a non-stick skillet, brown the onions and garlic in 1 tablespoon oil over medium heat. Add rice, cumin, cardamom, cinnamon, rose petals, 1 teaspoon salt, and pepper. Cook for 5 minutes, stirring occasionally.

3. Add chicken broth; cover and simmer over low heat for 20 minutes.

4. Add barberries, almonds, raisins, and lime juice. Mix well and remove from heat.

5. Preheat the oven to 350°F. Stuff chicken with the rice mixture and truss the cavity shut.

6. Place chicken in a greased ovenproof dish or roasting pan. Mix saffron water and apple juice and pour over the chicken; cover with aluminum foil.

7. Place pan in the oven and roast for 1½ hours, basting occasionally with the pan juices. Cook until the meat separates easily from the bone.

8. Serve the chicken in the baking dish or on a serving platter. Garnish with lime slices and accompany with bread, *sabzi-khordan* and salad. *Nush-e Jan!*

Sweet and Sour Stuffed Quail with Rose Petals

Makes 4 servings
Preparation time: 45 minutes
Cooking time: 55 minutes

بلدرچین توپر

Belderchin-e tu por

8 quails, with all small bones removed from the cavity
1½ teaspoons salt
½ teaspoon freshly ground black pepper
1 large onion, peeled and thinly sliced
4 cloves garlic, peeled and crushed
1 tablespoon olive oil
1 large tomato, peeled and chopped
½ cup ground walnuts
¼ cup barberries, cleaned and washed (see note, page 61)

1 cup dried tart pitted cherries
¼ cup dried apricots or peaches
2 tablespoons sugar
¼ teaspoon cardamom
¼ teaspoon cinnamon
¼ teaspoon cumin
1 teaspoon dried rose petals
¼ cup fresh lime juice
1 cup freshly squeezed orange juice
½ teaspoon ground saffron, dissolved in 2 tablespoons hot water
Rose petals for garnish

Rose petals are as much part of Persian cooking as they are part of Persian literature.

1. Remove all the visible bones from the quail cavities; wash and pat dry.

2. Place the quail in a baking dish. Rub each bird inside and out with a mixture of ½ teaspoon salt and ¼ teaspoon pepper.

3. In a non-stick skillet, sauté the onion and garlic in 1 tablespoon oil over medium heat for 20 to 30 minutes. Add the tomato and continue cooking for five minutes.

4. Add walnuts, barberries, cherries, apricots (or peaches), sugar, 1 teaspoon salt, ¼ teaspoon pepper, cardamom, cinnamon, cumin, and rose petals. Mix well.

5. Preheat oven to 425°F.

6. Divide the stuffing into 8 portions. Stuff each quail and truss the cavity shut.

7. Mix lime juice, orange juice, and saffron water and pour over the quail. Bake for 20 to 25 minutes, basting occasionally.

8. When done, the quail should be golden. Arrange quail on a serving dish, garnished with rose petals, and serve with *chelow* (saffron steamed rice, page 88). *Nush-e jan!*

Sweet and Sour Stuffed Chicken

Makes 4 servings
Preparation time: 30 minutes
Cooking time: 1 hour 50 minutes

Morgh-e tu por-e torsh-o-shirin

2 Cornish game hens or 2 small frying chickens with skin removed
2½ teaspoons salt
1 tablespoon oil
1 large onion, peeled and thinly sliced
2 cloves garlic, peeled and crushed
1 cup pitted and finely chopped prunes

1 apple, cored and chopped
1 cup finely chopped dried apricots
½ cup raisins
¼ teaspoon freshly ground black pepper
1 teaspoon ground cinnamon
¼ teaspoon ground saffron, dissolved in 2 tablespoons hot water
1 teaspoon sugar
½ cup orange juice

This stuffing is excellent for turkey as well.

1. Clean and rinse the hens or chickens in cold water, then pat dry and rub with ½ teaspoon salt.

2. Heat oil in a non-stick skillet and brown onion and garlic. Add prunes, apple, apricots, raisins, 2 teaspoons salt, pepper, cinnamon, saffron water, and sugar. Mix well.

3. Preheat the oven to 350°F. Stuff the hens or chickens with the fruit mixture and truss the cavities shut.

4. Place the stuffed birds in a greased ovenproof dish or roasting pan and pour in the orange juice. Cover and bake in the oven for 1½ hours, basting with pan juices, until the meat separates easily from bone.

5. Serve from the ovenproof dish or arrange the birds on a serving platter. Serve with *chelow* (saffron steamed rice, page 88), bread, salad and fresh herbs. *Nush-e Jan!*

Sautéed Shrimp with Herbs and Tamarind

Makes 4 servings
Preparation time: 25 minutes
Cooking time: 40 minutes

میگو با تمر هندی

Maygoo ba tamr-e hendi

1 large onion, peeled and thinly sliced
4 cloves garlic, peeled and crushed
4 tablespoons olive oil
1 large tomato, peeled and crushed
1 cup fresh chopped coriander leaves
3 tablespoons dried fenugreek
¼ cup fresh basil, chopped
¼ cup coarsely chopped walnuts

2 teaspoons curry powder
¼ teaspoon freshly ground black pepper
½ teaspoon ground cinnamon
¼ teaspoon ground cumin
½ teaspoon ground cardamom
1 teaspoon dried rose petals
⅔ cup tamarind liquid
1 pound raw peeled shrimp

1. In a non-stick skillet, brown the onion and garlic in 2 tablespoons olive oil over medium heat. Add tomato and continue cooking for 5 minutes.

2. Add coriander, fenugreek, basil, walnuts, curry powder, pepper, cinnamon, cumin, cardamom, rose petals, and tamarind liquid. Mix well and simmer over low heat for 20 minutes.

3. Cut the shrimp in half; wash and pat dry.

4. In a non-stick skillet, heat the rest of the olive oil and fry the shrimp for 5 minutes. Add to the sauce, cover and simmer over low heat for 10 minutes.

5. Add salt to taste and adjust seasoning. Serve with *chelow* (saffron steamed rice, page 88). *Nush-e Jan!*

Stuffed Fish with Pomegranate Sauce

Makes 4 servings
Preparation time: 15 minutes
Cooking time: 50 minutes

هی تو پر با نار

Mahi-ye tu por ba anar

1 large or 2 pounds firm-fleshed white fish, about ½ inch thick: John Dory, sea bass or halibut
1 teaspoon salt
1 tablespoon olive oil
1 onion, peeled and thinly sliced
3 cloves garlic, peeled and crushed
¼ teaspoon freshly ground black pepper
¼ cup chopped walnuts
1 cup pomegranate juice or 3 tablespoons pomegranate paste

1 tablespoon angelica powder (*gol-par*)
1 tablespoon candied orange peel (page 185)
½ teaspoon ground saffron, dissolved in 2 tablespoons hot water
2 tablespoons fresh lime juice
3 tablespoons pomegranate seed for garnish

1. Rinse fish in cold water. Pat dry with paper towel and rub both sides with 1 teaspoon salt.

2. Heat 1 tablespoon oil in a large non-stick pan and sauté onion and garlic over medium heat for 20 minutes. Add all the ingredients except the saffron water, lime juice and pomegranate seeds and simmer for 3 minutes. Mix well and remove from the heat.

3. Preheat the oven to 400°F. Place the fish in a baking dish, stuff the fish with the mixture from step 2 and pin the cavity shut. Pour the saffron water and lime juice over the fish.

4. Place the fish in the oven and bake for 10 to 15 minutes (until the fish flakes easily with a fork), basting from time to time.

5. Arrange the fish on a serving platter. Pour the sauce from the baking dish over the fish. Sprinkle the pomegranate seeds over the fish.

6. Serve with *chelow* (saffron-steamed rice, page 88). *Nush-e Jan!*

Variation: Replace the pomegranate juice or paste with 1 cup liquid tamarind.

Grilled Fish with Sumac

1 whole or 4 thick firm-fleshed white fish fillets of John Dory, red snapper, sea bass, salmon, rockfish, swordfish, or orange roughy
1 teaspoon salt

¼ teaspoon freshly ground black pepper
Juice of 1 lime
½ cup sumac powder
2 tablespoons olive oil

Makes 4 servings
Preparation time: 10 minutes
plus 3 hours' marinating time
Cooking time: 5 to 7 minutes

Kabab-e mahi ba somaq

1. Wash the fish and pat dry with a paper towel. Rub it well with 1 teaspoon salt and ¼ teaspoon pepper. Place it in a baking dish.

2. Squeeze lime juice over fish. Sprinkle both sides of the fillets with sumac powder to completely cover. Let stand, covered, in refrigerator for 3 hours.

3. Preheat the broiler. Uncover the fish and pour 2 tablespoons of oil over it. Broil in the upper level of the broiler for 3 to 4 minutes on each side, or grill the fish over hot coals for approximately 6 to 10 minutes on both sides.

4. Serve with *chelow* (saffron steamed rice, page 88). *Nush-e Jan!*

Smoked White Fish

1 whole Canadian smoked white
    fish, 4–5 pounds
3 cloves garlic, peeled and crushed
4 fresh limes or Seville oranges
    (2 for juicing, 2 cut in half for
    garnish)

3 whole bulbs garlic with the skin
2 tablespoons olive oil, diluted in
    ⅓ cup water
½ teaspoon salt
¼ teaspoon pepper
3 sprigs of thyme

Makes 6 servings
Preparation time: 10 minutes
Cooking time: 1 hour

Mahi-ye doodi

1. Preheat oven to 350°F. Place the fish in the center of a baking dish and stuff the fish with 3 cloves crushed garlic and the juice of 2 limes or Seville oranges. Place the garlic bulbs around the fish and sprinkle with olive oil, salt, pepper, and thyme.

2. Wrap aluminum foil loosely around the dish. Place the baking dish in the preheated oven and bake for 1 hour.

3. Remove fish from oven and gently transfer to a serving dish. Garnish with whole garlic and limes or Seville oranges. *Nush-e Jan!*

Sautéed Fish with Garlic and Seville Orange

4 thick fillets of red snapper, orange
   roughy, rockfish, or salmon
2 tablespoons all-purpose flour
1 teaspoon salt
10 cloves garlic, peeled
4 tablespoons olive oil
½ teaspoon ground turmeric
   or saffron

¼ teaspoon freshly ground
   black pepper
½ cup defatted fish broth
1 cup Seville orange juice or mixture
   of ½ cup fresh squeezed orange
   juice and ¼ cup lime juice

Makes 4 servings
Preparation time: 10 minutes
Cooking time: 30 minutes

ماهی سیر داغ با نارنج

*Mahi-e sir-dagh
ba narenj*

1. Wash and pat fish dry. Dust with 1 tablespoon flour and 1 teaspoon salt.

2. In a large non-stick skillet, sauté fish and garlic on both sides in 2 tablespoons olive oil over medium heat.

3. Add the turmeric and pepper; sauté for a few minutes, until golden brown. Add the fish broth.

4. Dissolve 1 tablespoon flour in the Seville orange juice; add this to the skillet. Salt and pepper to taste.

5. Simmer for another 10 minutes or until fish is tender.

6. Remove from heat; place the fish on a serving platter. Pour the sauce over it and serve with *chelow* (saffron-steamed rice, page 88), fresh herbs, and *torshi* (Persian pickles). *Nush-e Jan!*

Fish Stuffed with Fresh Herbs

Makes 6 servings
Preparation time: 30 minutes
Cooking time: 30–45 minutes,
depending on the size of fish

ماهی تو پُر با سبزی

Mahi-ye tu por ba sabzi

1 large fish (sea bass, salmon, rock-fish) or 6 thick fillets of flounder or orange roughy, about 6 pounds total, cleaned and scaled
2 teaspoons salt
3 tablespoons olive oil
2 cloves garlic, peeled and crushed
½ cup chopped fresh parsley
2 tablespoons chopped fresh tarragon
4 scallions, chopped
1 tablespoon chopped fresh coriander
¼ cup chopped fresh mint or 2 tablespoons dried

1 cup finely ground walnuts
¼ cup dried barberries, cleaned, soaked for 20 minutes in water and drained
¼ cup raisins
¼ cup fresh lime juice
¼ teaspoon freshly ground black pepper
½ teaspoon ground saffron, dissolved in 2 tablespoons hot water
1 lime or 2 Seville oranges, cut in half

1. Rinse fish in cold water. Pat dry with paper towel and rub inside and out with 1 teaspoon salt.

2. In a non-stick skillet, heat 2 tablespoons of oil and sauté garlic, parsley, tarragon, scallions, coriander, and mint; add walnuts, barberries, raisins, lime juice, 1 teaspoon salt, and pepper. Mix well and remove from heat.

3. Preheat oven to 400°F. Fill the fish with the herb stuffing; pin the cavity shut. Lay the fish in a greased baking dish. Dot the fish with the remaining oil and saffron water; place in the oven. Bake for 20 to 30 minutes (depending on the size of the fish), until the fish flakes easily with a fork. Baste occasionally with pan juices.

4. Arrange the fish on a serving platter and garnish with lime or Seville orange slices.

5. Serve with *chelow* (saffron-steamed rice, page 88) and fresh herbs. *Nush-e Jan!*

Notes: If using fish fillets, place the stuffing in the center of a greased baking dish. Cover it with fish and pour the saffron water, oil, and juice over the fish. Continue with step 4.

Clean sand from dried barberries (*zereshk*) by removing their stems and placing barberries in a colander. Place colander in a large container full of cold water and allow barberries to soak for 20 minutes. The sand will settle to the bottom of the container. Take the colander out of the container and run cold water over the barberries; drain and set aside. If using fresh barberries, remove stems and rinse with cold water.

Stuffed Sweet and Sour Fish

Makes 4 servings
Preparation time: 15 minutes
Cooking time: 30 minutes

1 large fish (sea bass) or 6 thick fillets of flounder or orange roughy, cleaned and scaled
2 teaspoons salt
4 tablespoons olive oil
½ cup finely chopped scallions
2 cloves garlic, peeled and crushed
¼ cup pitted and chopped dates
¼ cup finely chopped dried apricots
⅓ cup slivered pistachios
⅓ cup slivered blanched almonds

1 tablespoon candied orange peel (page 185)
Juice of 3 limes
½ teaspoon ground cinnamon
¼ teaspoon freshly ground black pepper
¼ teaspoon ground saffron, dissolved in 2 tablespoons hot water

Garnish
2 tablespoons toasted slivered almonds and pistachios

Mahi-ye tu por-e torsh-o shirin

1. Rinse fish in cold water. Pat dry with paper towel and rub inside and out with 1 teaspoon salt.

2. In a large non-stick frying pan, heat 2 tablespoons olive oil and sauté scallions and garlic. Add dates, apricots, pistachios, almonds, candied orange peel, juice of 1 lime, cinnamon, 1 teaspoon salt, and pepper. Mix well. Cook for 3 minutes.

3. Preheat the oven to 400°F. Stuff the fish with the mixture from step 2 and pin the cavity shut. Lay the fish in a greased baking dish. Pour the saffron water and the rest of the oil and lime juice over the fish.

4. Place in the oven and bake for 15 to 25 minutes, basting from time to time with the pan juices, until the fish flakes easily with a fork.

5. Arrange the fish on a serving platter or serve from the baking dish; sprinkle a few toasted slivered almonds and pistachios over it. Pour the juices from the baking dish over the fish.

6. Serve with *chelow* (saffron steamed rice, page 88). *Nush-e Jan!*

Ground Beef or Chicken Kabab

Makes 6 servings
Preparation time: 40 minutes
Cooking time: 10 minutes

کباب کوبیده

Kabab-e kubideh

For Beef Kabab
2 pounds lean ground beef
1 large onion, peeled and grated
1 tablespoon low-fat yogurt
1 teaspoon salt
¼ teaspoon freshly ground
    black pepper

Baste
2 tablespoons olive oil or melted
    butter
3 teaspoons powdered sumac

1 12-ounce package of *lavash* **bread**

For Chicken Kabab
2 pounds ground boneless lean
    chicken breast
1 small onion, peeled and grated
5 cloves garlic, peeled and grated
1 teaspoon salt
¼ cup olive oil

Garnish
½ cup sumac powder
2 limes, cut in half

1 12-ounce package of *lavash* **bread**

1. In a mixing bowl, combine beef or chicken and the rest of the ingredients. Blend in a mixer on medium speed or knead with your hands for 15 minutes to form a paste that will adhere well to cooking skewers. Cover the paste and let stand for 15 minutes at room temperature.

2. Start charcoal at least 30 minutes before you want to cook and let it burn until the coals are glowing evenly. (You can use a hair dryer to speed up this process.)

3. For the baste, melt the butter in a small saucepan and add a pinch of salt.

4. Using damp hands, divide the meat paste into 12 equal lumps about the size of oranges. Roll each into a sausage shape 5 inches long and mold it firmly around a flat, sword-like skewer.

5. Paint the kababs with melted butter or oil and arrange the skewers on the grill 3 inches above the coals; after a few seconds, turn the meat gently to help it attach to the skewers and to prevent it from falling off.

6. Grill the meat 3 to 5 minutes on each side, brushing occasionally with oil or butter. Avoid overcooking it. The meat should be seared on the outside, juicy and tender on the inside.

7. Spread *lavash* bread on a serving platter. Slide the meat off the skewer with another piece of bread. Arrange the meat on the bread, sprinkle with sumac or lime juice to taste, and cover meat with more *lavash* bread to keep it warm. Serve immediately with *chelow* (saffron steamed rice, page 88) or bread, fresh herbs, scallions, salad, *mast-o khiar* (yogurt and cucumbers), and *torshi* (Persian pickles). *Nush-e Jan!*

Baked Lamb

5–6 pounds leg of lamb, trimmed
   with all visible fat removed
1 bulb garlic, peeled
1 tablespoon salt
¼ teaspoon freshly ground
   black pepper
1 teaspoon turmeric
2 large onions, peeled and sliced
2 teaspoons ground rose petals

1½ teaspoons ground cinnamon
1½ teaspoons ground cumin
1½ teaspoons ground cardamom
1 teaspoon ground saffron dissolved
   in ¼ cup hot water
¼ cup fresh squeezed lime juice
3 tablespoons candied orange peel
   (page 185)
Rose petals for garnish

Makes 6-8 servings
Preparation time: 20 minutes
Cooking time: 4 hours

Khorak-e bareh

1. Rinse lamb and pat dry. Using the point of a small knife, make 10 slits all over the leg of lamb and insert a peeled clove of garlic in each slit. Rub salt, pepper and the turmeric all over the lamb. Heat a large non-stick skillet and brown all sides of the lamb over medium heat. Add onion and fry over medium heat until the onion becomes translucent.

2. Preheat oven to 350°F. Transfer the lamb and onion to an ovenproof baking dish. Sprinkle the salt, pepper, rose petals, cinnamon, cumin, cardamom, candied orange peel and saffron water all over the lamb. Pour ¼ cup fresh lime juice and ¼ cup water over the lamb.

3. Cover the lamb with aluminum foil and roast it for 3½ hours, basting occasionally with pan juice. Uncover the lamb for the last 30 minutes of cooking. Use a meat thermometer to ensure that the lamb is well-cooked. A well-done lamb tends to be more tender.

4. When done, place the lamb on a board and garnish with rose petals. Slice and serve along with *chelow* (saffron steamed rice, page 88). *Nush-e Jan!*

Rice Meatballs

Makes 6 meatballs
Preparation time: 35 minutes
Cooking time: 1 hour 30 minutes

کوفته برنجی

Kufteh berenji

Note: If you must use dried herbs, reduce the measurement to ¼ of the fresh herbs. Place the dried herbs in a sieve in a bowl of lukewarm water and allow to soak for 15 minutes. Remove the sieve and use the herbs as per the recipe.

½ cup yellow split peas
1 cup rice, cleaned and washed
2 teaspoons salt
2 egg whites
½ teaspoon ground rose petals
½ teaspoon ground cardamom
½ teaspoon ground cumin
½ teaspoon ground cinnamon
¼ teaspoon freshly ground
    black pepper
3 large onions, 1 peeled and grated
    and 2 peeled and thinly sliced
1 pound lean ground meat (lamb,
    veal, or beef)
2 cups chopped fresh parsley
1 cup chopped fresh dill
½ cup chopped fresh summer
    savory or 2 tablespoons dried

¼ cup chopped fresh tarragon or
    1 tablespoon dried
2 cups fresh chopped chives
    or scallions
2 cloves garlic, peeled and crushed
2 tablespoons olive oil
1 cup tomato juice
2 cups water
2 cups homemade defatted beef
    broth (page 27)
1 cup unripe plums (*gojeh sabz*) or
    ¼ cup fresh lime juice
1 teaspoon turmeric
¼ teaspoon ground saffron, dis-
    solved in 1 tablespoon hot water

1. Cook split peas and rice in a saucepan in 4 cups water with ½ teaspoon salt over medium heat for 30 minutes. Drain, reserving the juices, and set aside to cool.

2. Place egg whites in a mixing bowl; add ½ teaspoon salt, rose petals, cardamom, cumin, cinnamon, and pepper and beat well. Add the grated onion, ground meat, chopped parsley, dill, summer savory, tarragon, scallions, split peas, and rice. Knead the mixture thoroughly for about 10 minutes (at medium speed if using a mixer) until it has the consistency of a smooth paste.

3. In a heavy pot, brown the 2 remaining onions and garlic in the oil. Add tomato juice, water, beef broth, juice from the rice and split peas, unripe plums or ¼ cup lime juice, turmeric, 1 teaspoon salt, and saffron water. Bring to a boil.

4. Shape meat paste into balls the size of oranges. Gently place the meatballs into the boiling pot of broth. Cover partially and simmer gently for 45 minutes over low heat, basting the meatballs occasionally with the broth to prevent them from drying out.

5. Cover and simmer over low heat for 15 minutes longer.

6. Check to see if pan liquids have thickened, and adjust salt to taste. Place the meatballs in a bowl and gently pour the pan sauce on top. Serve hot with yogurt and bread. *Nush-e Jan!*

Variation: You may replace the lime juice with 2 tablespoons curry powder or 2 tablespoons sumac powder or 1 cup tart cherries

R I C E

Types of Cooked Rice

Kateh is the traditional dish of the Iranian province of Gilan, by the Caspian Sea. It is the simplest way of cooking Persian rice. Rice, water, and salt are cooked until the water is absorbed. Butter is added, the pot is covered, and the rice is allowed to cook. The rice becomes compact with a crusty surface. In the Caspian region, *kateh* is eaten for breakfast heated with milk and jam, or served cold with cheese and garlic. For lunch and dinner it is eaten with meat, fowl, fish, or *khoresh* (stew). *Damy* is similar to *kateh* except that it is cooked with herbs and vegetables, and once the rice begins to boil the heat is reduced to very low and the pot is covered immediately with a lid wrapped with 2 layers of paper towel or a dish towel (*dam-koni*).

Chelow has the same ingredients as *kateh* except that more care is taken in the cooking process, including presoaking, parboiling, and steaming. This results in a fluffy rice with each grain separate, and the bottom of the pot has a crisp golden brown crust, *tah dig. Tah dig* should be a golden color, never scorched or dark brown. The reputation of Iranian cooks rests on the quality of their *tah dig*, or golden crust. *Chelow* is then eaten with *khoresh*, called *chelow-khoresh*, or with *kabab, called chelow-kabab*.

Polow is initially cooked in the same way as *chelow*, but the meat, fruit, and vegetables are fried together and arranged in alternating layers with the rice, and then steamed together.

Rice is, of course, also used in many other dishes in Persian cuisine, including soups, *ashes*, meatballs, *kufte-berenji*, stuffed vegetables, and *dolmeh*. There are also many sweets and cookies made using rice flour: *halva, fereni, shirberenj*, and *nan-e berenji*. Rice is also popped in a way similar to making popcorn (*berenj-e budadeh* or *berenjak)*, and deep-fried as a candy, *reshteh bereshteh*.

A Note on Cleaning, Washing and Soaking Rice

Basmati rice contains many small, solid particles. This grit must be removed by picking over the rice carefully by hand. Then the rice must be washed thoroughly in warm water. Place the rice in a large pot and cover with warm water. Agitate gently with your hand, without breaking the rice, then pour off the water. Repeat 5 times until the rice is completely clean. When washed rice is cooked, it gives off a delightful perfume that unwashed rice does not have. In Gilan, large quantities of rice are often soaked in saltwater and used for cooking as needed. Soaking and cooking in saltwater seems to help firm up the rice, lengthen it, and keep it separated and fluffy after the cooking process. For draining, an ordinary colander's holes may be too large and you may lose some of the rice; instead use a large freestanding mesh strainer or sieve.

Throughout this book I have used cooking times for basmati rice, which I recommend. If you use American long-grain rice it is not necessary to wash the rice 5 times, and cooking times may vary.

Pots for Cooking Rice

A deep, non-stick pot must be used to enable the rice grains to swell properly and for a good *tah dig* to form without sticking to the bottom. Rice cookers are a wonderful invention for cooking rice Persian-style because the non-stick coated mold allows for a golden crust (*tah dig*) and, as the temperature does not vary, it allows for consistently good rice. However, each type of rice cooker seems to have its own temperature setting; therefore the timing must be experimented with to get the best results. Step-by-step instructions are given for Steamed Plain Rice and Rice with Lentils using the National Delux electric rice cooker. Other rice recipes can be carried out similarly.

Saffron Steamed Basmati Rice

3 cups long-grain basmati rice
6 cups water
2 teaspoons salt
3 tablespoons olive oil
4 tablespoons plain low-fat yogurt
1 teaspoon ground saffron, dissolved in 4 tablespoons hot water

Makes 6 servings
Preparation time: 15 minutes
Cooking time: 1 hour

چِلُو

Chelow

Note: Saffron is the dried stamens of a crocus. It was used in ancient times as a medicine, for dyeing clothes and to enhance the color and flavor of food.

This is a master recipe that details certain steps applicable to all other rice recipes.

1. Clean by picking over the rice. Basmati rice like any other old rice contains many small solid particles. This grit must be removed by picking over the rice carefully by hand.

2. Wash the rice by placing it in a large container and covering it with lukewarm water. Agitate briskly with your hand, then pour off the water. Repeat five times until the rice is completely clean. When washed rice is cooked it gives off a delightful perfume that unwashed rice does not have. **If using long-grain American or Texmati rice, it is not necessary to soak or wash five times.** Cooking rice with salt firms it up to support the long cooking time and prevents the rice from breaking up. The grains swell individually without sticking together. The result is light and fluffy rice called Pearls of Persian Cuisine.

3. Bring 6 cups of water with 2 teaspoons salt to a boil in a large non-stick pot. Pour the washed and drained rice into the pot. Boil briskly for 6 to 10 minutes; stir gently twice with a wooden spoon to loosen any grains that may have stuck to the bottom. Bite a few grains. If the rice feels soft, it is ready. Drain rice in a large free-standing strainer or sieve.

4. In the same pot, heat 2 tablespoons oil, two full spatulas of rice, 4 tablespoons yogurt, and 1 tablespoon saffron water; spread this mixture over the bottom of the pot and even out with back of a spatula. This will help to make a golden crust (*tah dig*).

5. Take one spatula full of rice at a time and gently place it on top of the bottom layer, gradually shaping the rice into a pyramid. This shape leaves room for the rice to expand and enlarge. Poke 1 or 2 holes in the rice pyramid with the handle of a wooden spoon.

6. Cover and cook rice for 10 minutes over medium heat in order to form a golden crust.

7. Dissolve 1 tablespoon oil in ½ cup hot water and pour over the rice pyramid. Place a clean dish towel or 2 layers of paper towel over the pot and cover firmly with the lid to prevent steam from escaping. Cook for 50 minutes longer over low heat.

8. Remove the pot from heat. Allow to cool on a damp surface for 5 minutes without uncovering it. This helps to free the crust from the bottom of the pot. Then put 2 tablespoons of rice in a dish, mix with remaining saffron water, and set aside for garnish.

9. Gently taking one spatula full of rice at a time, place it on a serving platter without disturbing the crust. Mound the rice into a cone. Sprinkle the saffron rice garnish over the top. For a tastier effect, you may melt 2 tablespoons butter and drizzle over the rice.

10. Detach the layer of crust from the bottom using a wooden spatula. Place on a small platter and serve on the side or arrange it around the rice. *Nush-e Jan!*

Saffron Steamed Plain Rice: Rice Cooker Method

3 cups long-grain basmati rice
3½ cups water
1 teaspoon salt
2 tablespoons olive oil
¼ teaspoon ground saffron, dissolved in 1 tablespoon hot water

Makes 6 servings
Preparation time: 10 minutes
Cooking time: 1 hour 30 minutes

چلو با پلوپز

Chelow ba polow paz

Saffron is the dried stamens of a crocus. It was used in ancient times as a medicine, for dyeing clothes and to enhance the color and flavor of food.

1. Pick over and wash 3 cups of rice 5 times in warm water.

2. Combine all the ingredients except the saffron water in the rice cooker; gently stir with a wooden spoon and start the cooker.

3. After 1½ hours, pour saffron water on top of rice. Unplug rice cooker.

4. Allow to cool for 10 minutes without uncovering the pot.

5. Remove lid and place a round serving dish over the pot. Hold the dish and the pot tightly together and turn them over to unmold rice. The rice will be like a cake. Cut into wedges and serve. *Nush-e Jan!*

Note: These cooking times are for the National Delux rice cooker. The cooking time for rice may vary according to different brands of rice cookers. It is desirable but not essential to soak the rice in 8 cups water with 2 tablespoons salt for 2 to 24 hours. This is especially good for older basmati-type rice. For American long-grain rice, use only 3 cups of water and wash the rice once. Among other long-grain types of rice, choose those that are long, thick, and sleek at the tip.

Smothered Rice

3 cups long-grain basmati rice
2 teaspoons salt
5½ cups water
2 tablespoons olive oil

Makes 6 servings
Preparation time: 5 minutes
Cooking time: 1 hour

Kateh

1. Pick over and wash 3 cups of rice 5 times in warm water.

2. Place rice, salt, and water in a deep non-stick pot. Bring to a boil over high heat, then reduce heat and simmer for 15 to 20 minutes over medium heat (do not cover the rice). Gently stir the rice with a wooden spoon a few times while it boils.

3. When the rice has absorbed all the water, pour the oil over it and stir through gently with a wooden spoon. Reduce heat.

4. Place a clean dish towel or 2 layers of paper towel over the pot and cover firmly with the lid on to prevent steam from escaping. Cook 40 minutes over low heat. Remove the pot from heat and allow to cool for 5 minutes on a damp surface without uncovering.

5. Gently taking one skimmer or spatula full of rice at a time, without disturbing the bottom crust, place the rice on a serving platter. Mound rice in shape of a cone.

6. Detach the crust from the bottom of the pot using a wooden spatula. Place on a small platter and serve on the side. *Nush-e Jan!*

Rice with Lentils

Makes 6 servings
Preparation time: 35 minutes
Cooking time: 1 hour 25 minutes

عدس پلو

Adas polow

3 cups long-grain basmati rice
1½ cups lentils
½ teaspoon salt
1 medium onion, peeled and thinly
   sliced
½ cup olive oil
1 cup raisins
2 cups pitted dates
2 tablespoons candied orange peel
   (page 185)

4 tablespoons low-fat yogurt
1 teaspoon ground saffron, dissolved in 4 tablespoons hot water
1 teaspoon ground cinnamon
1 teaspoon ground rose petals
½ teaspoon ground cardamom
¼ teaspoon ground cumin
¼ teaspoon ground cinnamon

1. Pick over and wash 3 cups of rice 5 times in lukewarm water.

2. Cook lentils about 10 minutes in 3 cups water and ½ teaspoon salt. Drain and set aside.

3. In a non-stick frying pan, lightly brown the onion in 2 tablespoons oil over medium heat. Add raisins, dates, and candied orange peel. Sauté a few minutes longer, mix well and set aside.

4. Bring 6 cups of water and 2 teaspoons salt to a boil in a large non-stick pot. Pour the washed rice into the pot. Boil briskly for 6 minutes, gently stirring twice to loosen any grains that may have stuck to the bottom. Drain rice in a large free-standing sieve or strainer.

5. In the same pot, heat 2 tablespoons oil, add 2 spatulas full of rice, the yogurt, and 1 tablespoon of saffron water and spread this mixture over the bottom of the pot to help make a golden crust (*tah dig*).

6. Place 2 spatulas full of rice in the pot. Mix the spices and sprinkle half of them over the rice. Add a spatula full of lentils, then some of the raisin-and-date mixture. Repeat, alternating layers of rice with raisins and dates, mounding the ingredients in the shape of a pyramid. Sprinkle the remaining spices on top.

7. Cover and cook the rice pyramid for 10 minutes over medium heat. Pour a mixture of 4 tablespoons oil and ½ cup of water and the remaining saffron water over the rice. Place a clean dish towel or 2 layers of paper towel over the pot and cover firmly with the lid to prevent steam from escaping. Cook for 50 minutes longer over low heat.

8. Remove the pot from heat and allow to cool for 5 minutes on a damp surface without uncovering.

9. Uncover the pot, take out 2 tablespoons of the saffron-flavored rice from the top, and set aside for garnishing. Gently taking 1 spatula full of rice at a time, without disturbing the bottom crust, place the rice on a serving platter. Mound the rice in the shape of a cone. Decorate with saffron-flavored rice.

10. Detach the crust from the bottom of pot using a wooden spatula. Unmold onto a small platter and serve on the side with *torshi* (Persian pickles) and fresh herbs. *Nush-e Jan!*

Rice with Noodles

3 cups long-grain basmati rice
½ pound toasted Persian noodles
   (*reshteh*), cut into 1-inch lengths
1 onion, peeled and thinly sliced
4 tablespoons olive oil
½ cup raisins
2 tablespoons candied orange peel
   (page 185)

2 cups pitted dates, cut in half
4 tablespoons low-fat yogurt
1 teaspoons ground saffron, dissolved in 4 tablespoons hot water
1 teaspoon ground rose petals
½ teaspoon ground cardamom
¼ teaspoon ground cumin
¼ teaspoon ground cinnamon

Makes 6 servings
Preparation time: 15 minutes
Cooking time: 1 hour 20 minutes

Reshteh polow

1. Pick over and wash 3 cups of rice 5 times in warm water.

2. If not already toasted, toast noodles in a large skillet for few minutes until golden brown, or place on a cookie sheet and broil for 30 seconds.

3. In a non-stick skillet, brown the onion in 1 tablespoon oil over medium heat. Add the raisins, orange peel and dates. Sauté for a few minutes and set aside.

4. Bring 8 cups of water and 3 teaspoons salt to a boil in a large non-stick pot. Pour the washed and drained rice into the pot. Add the noodles. Boil briskly for 6 to 10 minutes, gently stirring with a wooden spoon twice to loosen any grains that may have stuck to the bottom. Drain rice in a large free-standing sieve or strainer.

5. In the same pot, heat 1 tablespoon oil. Add 2 spatulas full of rice, the yogurt, and 1 tablespoon saffron water and spread this mixture over the bottom of the pot to help make a golden crust (*tah dig*).

6. Place 2 spatulas full of the rice and noodle mixture in the pot. Mix the spices and sprinkle half of them over the rice. Add a spatula of the raisins, orange peel and dates. Repeat, arranging the rice in the shape of a pyramid. Sprinkle the remaining spices on top.

7. Cover and cook rice for 10 minutes over medium heat. Pour a mixture of 2 tablespoons oil, ½ cup water, and the remaining saffron water over the pyramid. Place a clean dish towel or two layers of paper towel over the pot and cover firmly with lid to prevent steam from escaping. Cook 50 minutes longer over low heat.

8. Remove rice from heat and allow to cool for 5 minutes on a damp surface without uncovering. This helps free the crust from the bottom of the pot.

9. Uncover the pot, take out 2 tablespoons of the saffron-flavored rice from the top, and set aside for garnishing. Gently taking 1 spatula full of rice at a time, without disturbing the bottom crust, place the rice on a serving platter. Mound the rice in the shape of a cone. Decorate with saffron-flavored rice.

10. Detach the crust from the bottom of the pot using a wooden spatula. Unmold onto a small platter and serve on the side with Persian pickles (*torshi*) and fresh herbs. *Nush-e Jan!*

Rice with Apricots

3 cups long-grain basmati rice
1 pound boned leg of lamb or
    chicken, cut in 1-inch cubes
1 onion, peeled and thinly sliced
2¼ cups dried apricots
½ cup raisins
½ cup pitted dates

5 tablespoons olive oil
1 teaspoon ground saffron, dis-
    solved in 2 tablespoons hot water
4 tablespoons low-fat yogurt
1 teaspoon ground rose petals
½ teaspoon ground cardamom
¼ teaspoon ground cinnamon

Makes 6 servings
Preparation time: 15 minutes
Cooking time: 1 hour 20 minutes

Gheisi polow

1. Pick over and wash 3 cups of rice 5 times in warm water.

2. In a non-stick skillet, brown meat and onion in 1 tablespoon oil over medium heat. Add apricots and 1½ cups water, cover and simmer for 40 minutes over low heat. Add the raisins and dates and set aside.

3. Bring 6 cups water and 2 teaspoons salt to a boil in a large non-stick pot. Pour the washed and drained rice into the pot. Boil briskly for 6 to 10 minutes, stirring gently with a wooden spoon twice to loosen any grains that may have stuck to the bottom. Drain rice in a large free-standing sieve or strainer.

4. In the same pot, heat 2 tablespoons oil. Add 2 spatulas full of rice, the yogurt, and 1 tablespoon saffron water and spread this mixture over the bottom of the pot to help make a golden crust (*tah dig*).

5. Place 2 spatulas full of rice in the pot. Add 1 spatula full of the mixture from step 2. Mix the spices and sprinkle half of them on the rice. Repeat, alternating the rice with the fruit in the shape of a pyramid, and sprinkle the remaining spices on top.

6. Cover and cook for 10 minutes over medium heat.

7. Mix the remaining oil and ½ cup water and pour over the rice, then add the remaining saffron water.

8. Place a clean dish towel or 2 layers of paper towel over the pot and cover firmly with lid to prevent steam from escaping. Cook another 50 minutes over low heat. Remove the pot from heat and allow to cool for 5 minutes on a damp surface without uncovering it.

9. Uncover the pot, remove 2 tablespoons of the saffron-flavored rice from the top and set aside for garnishing. Gently taking 1 spatula full at a time, without disturbing the bottom crust, and place rice on an oval serving platter. Mound the rice in the shape of a cone. Decorate with the saffron-flavored rice. Detach the crust from the bottom of the pot using a wooden spatula. Unmold onto a small platter and serve on the side with roasted lamb or chicken and fresh herbs.

Rice with Fresh Fava Beans

2 pounds fresh fava beans with the shell or 1 pound frozen
3 cups long-grain basmati rice
½ teaspoon turmeric
½ cup olive oil
4 tablespoons low-fat yogurt
1½ teaspoons ground saffron, dissolved in 2 tablespoons hot water

6 cups fresh dill weed, finely chopped
4 cloves garlic, peeled and chopped or 4 whole green garlic bulbs, trimmed
2 teaspoons ground cinnamon

Makes 6 servings
Preparation time: 20 minutes
Cooking time: 1 hour 15 minutes

Baqala polow

Notes: If you must use dried herbs, reduce the measurement to ¼ of the fresh herbs. Place the dried herbs in a sieve in a bowl of lukewarm water and allow to soak for 15 minutes. Remove the sieve and use the herbs as per the recipe.

You may substitute lima beans for fava beans. If you use baby lima beans, do not remove the skin.

1. Shell beans and remove outer layer of skin. If using frozen fava beans, soak in warm water for a few minutes, then peel.

2. Pick over and wash 3 cups basmati rice 5 times in warm water.

3. Bring 8 cups of water and 3 teaspoons salt to a boil in a large, non-stick pot. Pour the rice into the pot. When the water boils again, add the fava beans and turmeric to the pot while water is boiling (turmeric helps the greens stay green).

4. Boil briskly for 6 to 10 minutes, stirring gently a few times with a wooden spoon to loosen any stuck grains. Remove from heat and drain in a large freestanding sieve or strainer.

5. In the same pot, heat 2 tablespoons oil. Add 2 spatulas full of rice, the yogurt and 1 tablespoon saffron water and spread this mixture over the bottom of the pot to help make a golden crust (*tah dig*).

6. Place a spatula full of rice and beans in the pot, then a spatula of dill, then sprinkle some of the garlic and cinnamon over the rice. Repeat these layers, forming a pyramid shape. Cover and cook over medium heat for 10 minutes.

7. Mix the remaining oil and ½ cup warm water and pour over the rice pyramid. Add the remaining saffron water to the top.

8. Place a clean dish towel or 2 layers of paper towel over the pot; cover the pot tightly to prevent steam from escaping. Cook 50 minutes longer over low heat. Remove pot from heat; allow to cool on a damp surface without uncovering it.

9. Remove lid and take out 2 tablespoons of the saffron-flavored rice and set aside for garnish.

10. Gently taking 1 spatula of rice at a time, mound the rice in the shape of a pyramid on a serving platter. Garnish with the saffron-flavored rice.

11. Detach the crust from the bottom of the pot with a wooden spatula. Unmold onto a small platter and serve with yogurt or *torshi* (Persian pickles). This rice can also be served with roasted lamb or chicken. *Nush-e Jan!*

Jeweled Rice

Makes 6 servings
Preparation time: 40 minutes
Cooking time: 1 hours 40 minutes

جواهر پلو

Javaher polow

Notes: Clean barberries by removing their stems and placing the berries in a colander. Place colander in a large container full of cold water and allow barberries to soak for 20 minutes. The sand will settle to the bottom. Take the colander out of the container and run cold water over the barberries; drain and set aside.

Jeweled rice is often served at weddings. Each of the elements represents a desirable jewel; for example, barberries for rubies, pistachios for emeralds.

3 cups long-grain basmati rice
1 cup very finely slivered Seville orange peel
2 cups large carrots, peeled and cut into thin strips
1 cup sugar
1 small onion, thinly sliced
¼ cup olive oil
1 cup dried barberries (*zereshk*), cleaned, washed, and drained
½ cup raisins

4 tablespoons low-fat yogurt
1 teaspoon ground saffron, dissolved in 4 tablespoons hot water
1 teaspoon ground rose petals
½ teaspoon ground cardamom
¼ teaspoon ground cumin
¼ teaspoon ground cinnamon

Garnish
2 tablespoons slivered almonds
2 tablespoons slivered pistachios

1. Pick over and wash 3 cups of rice 5 times in warm water.

2. In a saucepan, cover the slivered orange peel with water, boil for 10 minutes over medium heat, and then drain to remove bitterness. Place the orange peel, carrot strips, 1 cup sugar, and 1 cup water in a large saucepan and simmer for 10 minutes over medium heat. Drain and reserve the syrup.

3. In a non-stick skillet, sauté the onion in 1 tablespoon oil over medium heat for 20 minutes until light golden in color. Add barberries and raisins and cook for just 1 minute because barberries burn very easily. Remove from heat and set aside.

4. Bring 6 cups water and 2 teaspoons salt to a boil in a large, non-stick pot. Pour the rice into the pot. Boil briskly for 6 minutes, gently stirring twice to loosen any grains that may have stuck to the bottom. Drain in a large free-standing sieve or strainer.

5. In the same pot, heat 2 tablespoons oil. Add 2 spatulas of rice, the yogurt and 1 tablespoon saffron water. Spread this mixture over the bottom of the pot to help make a golden crust (*tah dig*).

6. Place 2 spatulas full of rice in the pot, then add 1 spatula of orange peel and carrots. Mix the spices and sprinkle half of them over the rice. Repeat these steps, arranging the rice and orange-carrot mixture in layers in the shape of a pyramid. This shape allows room for the rice to expand and enlarge. Sprinkle the remaining spices over the rice. Cover and cook for 10 minutes over medium heat.

7. Mix the rest of the oil with ¼ cup water and ¼ cup of the reserved syrup and pour over the rice. Add saffron water. Place a clean dish towel or two layers of paper towel over the pot and cover firmly with the lid to prevent steam from escaping. Cook for 45 minutes longer over low heat. Remove from heat and allow to cool for 5 minutes on a damp surface, without uncovering. This helps free the crust from the bottom of the pot.

8. Remove lid and take out 2 tablespoons of saffron-flavored rice and set aside for use as garnish. Then, gently taking 1 spatula full of rice at a time, place rice on a serving platter in alternating layers with the barberry mixture. Mound the rice in the shape of a cone. Decorate the top of the mound with the saffron-flavored rice, some of the barberry mixture, and almonds and pistachios. Detach the crust from the bottom of the pot using a wooden spatula. Unmold onto a small platter and serve on the side.
Nush-e Jan!

Rice with Green Cabbage

Makes 6 servings
Preparation time: 30 minutes
Cooking time: 2 hours

Kalam-e polow

3 cups long-grain basmati rice
1 pound lean stewing meat (veal, beef, or chicken breast), cut into ½-inch cubes
1 onion, peeled and sliced
½ cup olive oil
½ teaspoon salt
¼ teaspoon freshly ground black pepper
6 medium tomatoes, peeled and chopped, or 3 cups tomato juice

1 large head green cabbage, washed and chopped in 1-inch cubes
4 tablespoons low-fat yogurt
1 teaspoon ground saffron, dissolved in 2 tablespoons hot water
1 teaspoon ground rose petals
½ teaspoon ground cardamom
1 teaspoon ground cumin
¼ teaspoon ground cinnamon

1. Pick over and wash 3 cups of rice 5 times in warm water.

2. In a non-stick pot, brown the meat and onion in 2 tablespoons oil over medium heat for 20 minutes. Add salt, pepper, and tomato or tomato juice. Cover and cook for 30 minutes longer over medium heat.

3. Lightly brown the cabbage in 1 tablespoon oil in a non-stick skillet, stirring occasionally to prevent burning. Add it to the meat and cook for 10 minutes longer. Set aside.

4. Bring 6 cups water and 2 teaspoons salt to a boil in a large non-stick pot. Pour the rice into the pot. Boil briskly for 6 to 10 minutes, stirring gently twice to loosen any grains that may have stuck to the bottom. Drain rice in a large free-standing sieve or strainer.

5. In a non-stick pot, heat 2 tablespoons oil. Add 4 tablespoons yogurt, 1 table-spoon saffron water, and 2 spatulas full of rice. Spread this mixture over the bottom of the pot to help make a golden crust (*tah dig*).

6. Place 2 spatulas full of rice in the pot, then add a layer of the cabbage-and-meat mixture. Repeat by alternating layers of rice and the cabbage-and-meat mixture in the shape of a pyramid. Mix the ground rose petals, cardamom, cumin and cinnamon and sprinkle between the layers.

7. Cover and cook for 10 minutes over medium heat to help form a golden crust.

8. Mix the remaining oil and saffron water and pour over the pyramid. Place a clean dish towel or 2 layers of paper towel over the pot and cover firmly with the lid to prevent steam from escaping. Cover and cook 50 minutes longer over low heat. Remove the pot from heat and allow to cool for 5 minutes on a damp surface without uncovering it.

9. Uncover and take out 2 tablespoons of saffron-flavored rice for use as a garnish. Then, gently taking 1 spatula full at a time, without disturbing the bottom crust, place rice on an oval serving platter. Mound the rice in the shape of a cone. Garnish with the saffroned rice. Detach the crust from the bottom of the pot using a wooden spatula. Unmold onto a small platter and serve on the side. *Nush-e Jan!*

Rice with Green Beans

Makes 6 servings
Preparation time: 45 minutes
Cooking time: 1 hour

لوبيا پلو

Lubia polow

3 cups long-grain basmati rice
1 large onion, peeled and thinly sliced
2 cloves garlic, peeled and crushed
1 pound stew meat (veal, beef, or boneless chicken), cut into ½-inch cubes, or 1 pound lean ground meat
4 tablespoons olive oil
1 pound sliced, peeled, canned tomatoes, drained, or 6 large fresh tomatoes, peeled and sliced
1½ pounds fresh green beans, cleaned and cut into ½-inch pieces
1 teaspoon ground cinnamon
1½ teaspoons salt
¼ teaspoon freshly ground black pepper
4 tablespoons low-fat yogurt
½ teaspoon ground saffron, dissolved in 2 tablespoons hot water
1 teaspoon ground rose petals
½ teaspoon ground cardamom
¼ teaspoon ground cumin
¼ teaspoon ground cinnamon
1 teaspoon dried Persian lime powder (powdered *limu-omani*)

1. Pick over and wash 3 cups of rice 5 times in warm water.

2. In a non-stick saucepan, lightly brown the onion, garlic, and meat over medium heat in 1 tablespoon oil for 20 minutes. Add tomatoes, green beans, cinnamon, 1 teaspoon salt, and ¼ teaspoon pepper. Cover and simmer over low heat for 40 minutes. (If using canned tomatoes, make sure they are completely drained. They must not have any sauce left.)

3. Bring 6 cups of water and 2 teaspoons salt to a boil in a large non-stick pot. Pour the washed and drained rice into the pot. Boil briskly for 6 to 10 minutes over high heat, gently stirring twice to loosen any grains that may have stuck to the bottom. Drain rice in a large free-standing sieve or strainer.

4. In the same pot, heat 2 tablespoons oil. Add yogurt, 2 spatulas of rice, and 1 tablespoon saffron water. Spread this mixture over the bottom of the pot to help make a golden crust (*tah dig*).

5. Place 2 spatulas full of rice in the pot; then add a layer of the green-bean-and-meat mixture. Repeat by alternating layers of rice and the green bean mixture in the shape of a pyramid. Mix the spices and dried lime powder and sprinkle between the layers. Cover and cook for 10 minutes over medium heat.

6. Pour the remaining saffron water and oil over the rice. Place a clean dish towel or 2 layers of paper towel over the pot and cover firmly with the lid to prevent steam from escaping. Cook 50 minutes longer over low heat. Remove the pot from heat and allow to cool for 5 minutes on a damp surface without uncovering it. This helps to free the crust from the bottom of the pot.

7. Uncover, take out 2 tablespoons of the saffron-flavored rice and set aside for garnishing. Then, gently taking 1 spatula full of rice at a time, without disturbing the bottom crust, place rice on serving platter. Mound the rice in the shape of a cone. Decorate with saffron-flavored rice. Detach the crust from the bottom of the pot using a wooden spatula. Unmold onto a small platter and serve on the side with fresh scallions, basil, and *torshi* (Persian pickles). *Nush-e Jan!*

Chelow Kabab (Rice with Meat Kabab)

Chelow kabab

Chelow Kabab is Iran's national dish, the equivalent of steak and potatoes in the United States. *Chelow kabab* is served everywhere from palaces to roadside stalls, but the best is probably sold in the bazaars, where it is served with a tin cloche covering the rice to keep it warm. The kababs are brought to the table by the waiter, who holds five or ten skewers in his left hand and a piece of bread in his right hand. He places a skewer of kabab directly on the rice and, holding it down with the bread, dramatically pulls out the skewer, leaving the sizzling kababs behind.

Chelow kabab consists of *chelow* (steamed rice) and *kabab*, skewers of lamb, veal, or beef cubes or ground meat marinated in saffron, onions, yogurt, and lime juice. Grilled tomatoes and raw onions are also an integral part of *chelow kabab*. The traditional way to serve *chelow kabab* is as follows:

Heap a pyramid of *chelow* on each plate. Add a dab of butter and sprinkle with a teaspoon of powdered sumac. Mix well.

Place the kababs (*kabab-e kubideh, kabab-e barg* or a combination of both, called *sultani,* which literally means kingly) and the grilled tomatoes on the rice.

Serve hot with trimmings such as *sabzi-khordan* (fresh herbs and scallions), *mast-o khiar* (yogurt and cucumber), *mast-o musir* (yogurt and shallots), and *torshi* (Persian pickles). *Chelow kabab* is often washed down with *dugh*, a yogurt drink with mint, but a Pepsi with *chelow kabab* on Fridays for lunch was the treat of our childhood.

The prudent cook should always keep some meat marinating in the refrigerator at home to serve to unexpected guests and hungry members of the family. Then while the *chelow* is cooking, the fire can be started and the kababs prepared. This is truly convenience cooking—simple, yet nutritious and delicious. Children too love *chelow kabab*.

Baked Saffron Yogurt Rice with Lamb or Chicken

Makes 6 servings
Preparation time: 1 hour 30 minutes plus 8 hours' marinating
Cooking time: 3 to 3 hours 30 minutes

Tah chin-e barreh

Notes: You may also use a large non-stick muffin mold to make individual portions. Pour 1 teaspoon oil into each mold, fill them as described in step 5 and bake for 1¼ to 1½ hours.

This recipe can also be made without any meat inside but with any of the kababs on the side instead, or simply on its own.

1 small onion, peeled and thinly sliced
4 cloves garlic, peeled and crushed
¼ teaspoon freshly ground black pepper
¼ teaspoon turmeric
1 teaspoon ground rose petals
½ teaspoon ground cardamom
¼ teaspoon ground cumin
¼ teaspoon ground cinnamon

1½ cups low-fat yogurt
1 egg yolk
½ teaspoon ground saffron, dissolved in 2 tablespoons hot water
2 tablespoons candied orange peel (page 185)
1 pound lean boned leg of lamb or chicken, cut into 2-inch cubes
3 cups long-grain basmati rice
½ cup olive oil

1. In the bowl of a food processor, combine onion, garlic, pepper, turmeric, rose petals, cardamom, cumin, cinnamon, yogurt, egg yolk, 1½ tablespoons saffron water and orange peel. Beat well for a few minutes to create a smooth texture. Add salt to taste and marinate meat in this mixture for 8 to 24 hours for best results.

2. Pick over and wash 3 cups of rice 5 times in warm water.

3. Bring 6 cups water and 2 teaspoons salt to a boil in a large non-stick pot. Pour the rice into the pot. Boil briskly for 6 minutes, gently stirring twice to loosen any grains that may have stuck to the bottom. Drain in a large free-standing sieve or strainer.

4. Preheat oven to 350°F. Remove meat from the marinade. Add half the rice to the marinade and mix well.

5. Heat 4 tablespoons oil in a non-stick baking dish. Add the mixture of rice and marinade, spreading it across the bottom and up the sides of the baking dish. Place the pieces of meat on top and cover with the remaining rice. Pour the remaining saffron water and oil over the rice. Pack firmly using a wooden spoon and cover with oiled aluminum foil.

6. Place baking dish in the center of the oven and bake 1¼ to 1½ hours, until the bottom turns golden brown.

7. Remove baking dish from oven. Allow to cool on a damp surface for 5 minutes (do not uncover). Then loosen the rice around the edges of the baking dish with the point of a knife. Place a large serving dish over the baking dish. Hold both dishes firmly together with two hands and turn them upside down.

8. Serve hot with fresh herbs, yogurt, and Persian pickles (*torshi*). *Nush-e Jan!*

Rice with Fresh Herbs

Makes 6 servings
Preparation time: 45 minutes
Cooking time: 1 hour

سبزی پلو

Sabzi polow

Note: If you must use dried herbs, reduce the measurement to ¼ of the fresh herbs. Place the dried herbs in a sieve in a bowl of lukewarm water and allow to soak for 15 minutes. Remove the sieve and use the herbs as per the recipe.

3 cups long-grain basmati rice
4 tablespoons olive oil
4 tablespoons low-fat yogurt
½ teaspoon ground saffron, dissolved in 4 tablespoons hot water
½ cup chopped fresh chives or scallions
2 cups coarsely chopped fresh dill
2½ cups coarsely chopped fresh parsley
2 cups chopped fresh coriander
3 whole cloves garlic, peeled and crushed; and 3 whole cloves garlic or green garlic, washed thoroughly and trimmed
1 teaspoon ground cinnamon

This dish is associated with the New Year celebration.

1. Pick over and wash 3 cups of rice 5 times in lukewarm water.

2. Bring 6 cups of water and 2 teaspoons salt to a boil in a large non-stick pot. Pour the rice into the pot. Boil briskly for 6 minutes, gently stirring twice to loosen any grains that may have stuck to the bottom. Drain rice in a large free-standing sieve or strainer.

3. In the same pot, heat 2 tablespoons oil. Add 2 spatulas full of rice, yogurt, and one tablespoon saffron water. Spread this mixture over the bottom of the pot to help make a golden crust (*tah dig*).

4. Place 2 spatulas full of rice in the pot, then add one spatula full of herbs and all of the crushed and whole garlic. Repeat, alternating layers of the rice and herbs in the shape of a pyramid, and sprinkle the cinnamon between the layers. This shape allows room for the rice to expand and enlarge. Cover and cook for 10 minutes over medium heat.

5. Pour a mixture of 2 tablespoons oil and ½ cup hot water over this pyramid. Add the remaining saffron water on the top.

6. Place a clean dish towel or paper towel over the pot and cover firmly with the lid to prevent steam from escaping. Cook 45 minutes longer over low heat.

7. Remove pot from heat without uncovering and allow to cool for 5 minutes on a damp surface.

8. Uncover pot and set aside 2 tablespoons of saffron-flavored rice for garnish. Gently taking 1 spatula full of rice at a time, without disturbing the bottom crust, place the rice on a serving platter. Mound the rice in the shape of a cone. Decorate with saffron-flavored rice.

9. Detach the crust from the bottom of the pot using a wooden spatula. Unmold onto a small platter and serve on the side. Serve with any kind of fish, especially smoked white fish (page 73). *Nush-e Jan!*

Rice with Tart Cherries

3 cups dried red tart cherries*
¼ cup water
3 tablespoons sugar
1 teaspoon ground cinnamon
6 tablespoons corn oil
3 cups long-grain basmati rice
4 tablespoons low-fat yogurt

1 teaspoon ground saffron, dissolved in 2 tablespoons hot water

Garnish
1 tablespoon slivered almonds
2 tablespoons slivered pistachios
¼ cup cherry syrup

Makes 6 servings
Preparation time: 35 minutes
Cooking time: 1 hour

Albalu polow

*Note: If using sour, tart or Morello cherries in light syrup, use 3 jars (8 ounces each). Drain and discard syrup. Add 1 cup sugar, boil over medium heat for 30 minutes, drain and save the syrup.

If using sour cherries in heavy syrup, do not add sugar. Do not cook the sour cherries; just add ½ cup hot water to the cherries to dilute the syrup, then drain them for further use, because the syrup is too sweet to use on its own.

If using fresh or frozen pitted sour cherries, use ⅔ cup of sugar to each pound of cherries. Cook over high heat for 35 minutes, then drain.

1. Place cherries, water, sugar, and 2 tablespoons oil in a saucepan. Cook for 5 minutes over medium heat. Add cinnamon and set aside.

2. Pick over and wash 3 cups of rice 5 times in warm water.

3. Bring 6 cups water and 2 teaspoons salt to a boil in a large, non-stick pot. Pour the rice into the pot. Boil briskly for 6 minutes, gently stirring twice with a wooden spoon to loosen grains stuck together. Drain in a large free-standing sieve or strainer.

4. In the same pot, heat 2 tablespoons oil, add 4 tablespoons yogurt, 2 spatulas of rice and 1 tablespoon saffron water. Spread this mixture evenly over the bottom of the pot to help make a golden crust (*tah dig*).

5. Place 2 spatulas full of rice into the pot, then 1 spatula of cherries. Set aside 1 spatula full of cherries for garnish.

6. Repeat, alternating layers of rice and cherries in the shape of a pyramid.

7. Cover and cook over medium heat for 10 minutes. This will help form a crust on the bottom of the pan. Pour a mixture of 2 tablespoons oil and ¼ cup water over the pyramid. Pour the remaining saffron water over the top of the rice.

8. Place a dish towel or 2 layers of paper towel over the pot; cover firmly with the lid to prevent steam from escaping. Cook 45 minutes longer over low heat.

9. Remove the pot from heat without uncovering and allow to cool on a damp surface for 5 minutes. Take out 2 tablespoons of saffron-flavored rice and set aside with the rest of the garnish.

10. Gently taking 1 spatula at a time, without disturbing the bottom crust, place the rice on a platter. Mound rice in the shape of a pyramid. Garnish with the saffron rice, cherries, almonds, and pistachios. Pour ¼ cup hot cherry syrup over the rice. Detach crust from the bottom of the pot with a wooden spatula. Unmold onto a small platter and serve on the side. *Nush-e Jan!*

Carrot and Prune Khoresh

Makes 4 servings
Preparation time: 10 minutes
Cooking time: 1 hour 50 minutes

خورش هویج و آلو

Khoresh-e havij-o alu

1½ pounds chicken legs, cut up, with skin and all visible fat removed
2 tablespoons olive oil
2 medium onions, peeled and thinly sliced
1 clove garlic, peeled and crushed
1 teaspoon salt
¼ teaspoon freshly ground black pepper
1 teaspoon ground cinnamon
¼ teaspoon ground saffron, dissolved in 1 tablespoon hot water
¼ teaspoon ground cardamom
1 pound carrots, scraped and sliced
2 cups freshly squeezed orange juice
2 cups pitted prunes or golden plums (*alu zarb*)
2 tablespoons brown sugar
2 tablespoons lime juice

1. Heat a non-stick sauté pan and lightly brown chicken. Add 2 tablespoons oil, onion and garlic. Fry over medium heat, stirring occasionally, for 20 minutes or until onions become translucent. Add salt, pepper, cinnamon, saffron water, and cardamom.

2. Add carrots, orange juice, prunes, brown sugar and lime juice. Cover and simmer 1½ hours over low heat.

3. Check to see if chicken and prunes are tender. Taste the stew and adjust seasoning. Transfer to a deep ovenproof casserole. Cover and place in a warm oven until ready to serve.

4. Serve hot with *chelow* (saffron steamed rice, page 88). *Nush-e Jan!*

Butternut Squash and Prune Khoresh

Makes 4 servings
Preparation time: 35 minutes
Cooking time: 1 hour 40 minutes

خورش کدو حلوا و آلو

Khoresh-e kadu halvai-o alu

1½ pounds chicken legs, cut up, with skin and all excess fat removed
2 tablespoons olive oil
2 medium onions, peeled and thinly sliced
1 teaspoon salt
¼ teaspoon freshly ground black pepper
1 teaspoon ground cinnamon
2 cups pitted dried prunes or dried golden plums (*alu zard*)
2 pounds fresh butternut squash
3–4 tablespoons brown sugar
¼ cup fresh lime juice
¼ teaspoon ground saffron, dissolved in 1 tablespoon hot water

1. Heat a non-stick sauté pan and lightly brown chicken. Add 1 tablespoon oil and onion. Fry over medium heat, stirring occasionally, for 20 minutes or until onions become translucent. Add salt, pepper, cinnamon and prunes. Pour in 1 cup water. Cover and simmer over low heat for 30 minutes, stirring occasionally.

2. Meanwhile, peel and cut the squash into 2-inch cubes. Brown squash in 1 tablespoon oil in a non-stick skillet on all sides for 15 to 20 minutes over medium heat.

3. Add the brown sugar, lime juice, saffron water, and butternut squash cubes to the chicken. Cover and simmer 30 to 55 minutes over low heat.

4. Check the taste of the khoresh and adjust seasoning. Add more lime juice or sugar according to your taste.

5. In a deep casserole, carefully arrange first the butternut squash, then the chicken, and spoon in the broth. Cover and place in a warm oven. Serve hot from the same dish with *chelow* (saffron steamed rice, page 88). *Nush-e Jan!*

Variation: Chicken can be substituted with 1 pound lean stew meat (lamb, veal, or beef), cut up. In step 1, add 2 cups of water in place of 1 and simmer for 55 minutes instead of 30 minutes.

Artichoke Khoresh

Makes 4 servings
Preparation time: 25 minutes
Cooking time: 1 hour 45 minutes

1½ pounds chicken legs, cut up, with skin and all visible fat removed
2 tablespoons olive oil
2 medium onions, peeled and thinly sliced
1 teaspoon salt
¼ teaspoon freshly ground black pepper
½ teaspoon ground saffron, dissolved in 2 tablespoons hot water
¼ teaspoon turmeric
3 cups chopped fresh parsley
½ cup chopped fresh mint
5 tablespoons fresh lime juice or ¾ cup unripe grape juice (*ab ghureh*)
1 pound fresh, 2 packages frozen (9 ounces each), or 2 jars artichoke hearts, drained

Khoresh-e kangar

1. Heat a non-stick sauté pan and lightly brown chicken. Add 1 tablespoon oil and the onion. Fry over medium heat, stirring occasionally, for 20 minutes or until onion becomes translucent. Add salt, pepper, saffron water, and turmeric. Pour in 1½ cups water. Cover and simmer over low heat for 30 minutes, stirring occasionally.

2. In a non-stick skillet, fry the parsley and mint in 1 tablespoon oil over medium heat for 10 minutes and add to the chicken.

3. Add lime juice and the artichoke hearts to the chicken. Cover and simmer for 40 to 55 minutes over low heat.

4. Check to see if the artichoke hearts are tender. Taste the khoresh and adjust seasoning. Transfer it to a deep casserole. Cover and place in a warm oven until ready to serve.

5. Serve hot from the same dish with *chelow* (saffron steamed rice, page 88). *Nush-e Jan!*

Variation: Chicken can be replaced with 1 pound lean stew meat, (lamb, veal, or beef), cut into 1-inch cubes. In step 1, use 2½ cups of water in place of 1½ and simmer for 55 minutes instead of 30 minutes.

Celery Khoresh

Makes 4 servings
Preparation time: 30 minutes
Cooking time: 2 hours 25 minutes

Khoresh-e karafs

1½ pounds chicken legs, cut up, with skin and all visible fat removed
2 tablespoons olive oil
2 large onions, peeled and thinly sliced
1 teaspoon salt
½ teaspoon freshly ground black pepper
½ teaspoon turmeric

5 stalks celery, washed and chopped into 1-inch lengths (4 cups chopped)
3 cups chopped fresh parsley
½ cup chopped fresh mint or 2 tablespoons dried
½ cup fresh-squeezed lime juice or 1 cup unripe plums (*gojeh sabz*)
½ teaspoon ground saffron, dissolved in 2 tablespoons hot water

1. Heat a non-stick sauté pan and lightly brown chicken. Add 1 tablespoon oil and the onion. Fry over medium heat, stirring occasionally, for 20 minutes or until onion becomes translucent. Add salt, pepper, and turmeric. Pour in 1½ cups water. Cover and simmer over low heat for 15 minutes, stirring occasionally.

2. In a non-stick frying pan, fry the chopped celery in 1 tablespoon oil over medium heat for about 10 minutes, stirring occasionally with a wooden spoon. Add chopped herbs and continue to fry, stirring frequently with a wooden spoon, for another 10 to 15 minutes, or until the celery is golden brown.

3. Add the mixture of celery and herbs, the lime juice, and the saffron water to the chicken. Cover and simmer over low heat 1½ hours longer, or until the chicken and celery are tender.

4. Taste the stew and adjust seasoning accordingly. Transfer it to a deep casserole; cover and place in a warm oven until ready to serve.

5. Serve hot from the same dish with *chelow* (saffron steamed rice, page 88).

Nush-e Jan!

Variation: Chicken can be replaced with 1 pound lean stew meat, (lamb, veal or beef), cut in 1-inch cubes. In step 1, use 2½ cups of water in place of 1½ and simmer for 1 hour instead of 15 minutes.

Green Bean Khoresh

1½ pounds chicken legs, cut up, with skin and all visible fat removed
2 tablespoons olive oil
2 onions, peeled and thinly sliced
2 cloves garlic, peeled and crushed
1 teaspoon salt
¼ teaspoon freshly ground black pepper

1 teaspoon ground cinnamon
½ teaspoon turmeric
3½ cups fresh squeezed tomato juice
2 tablespoons fresh lime juice
1 pound fresh or frozen green beans, cut into 1-inch pieces
½ teaspoon saffron dissolved in 2 tablespoons hot water

Makes 4 servings
Preparation time: 30 minutes
Cooking time: 1 hour 50 minutes

Khoresh-e lubia sabz

1. Heat a non-stick sauté pan and lightly brown chicken. Add 1 tablespoon oil and the onion and garlic. Fry over medium heat, stirring occasionally with a wooden spoon, for 20 minutes or until onion becomes translucent. Add salt, pepper, cinnamon, and turmeric. Pour in tomato juice and lime juice. Cover and simmer for about 15 minutes over low heat, stirring occasionally.

2. Remove strings, if any, from beans. Cut into 1-inch pieces. Sauté in a non-stick skillet in 1 tablespoon oil.

3. Add green beans and saffron water to chicken. Cover and simmer 1 hour 15 minutes longer over low heat.

4. Taste and correct seasoning. Transfer the stew to an ovenproof casserole, cover, and place in a warm oven until ready to serve.

5. Serve hot from the same dish with *chelow* (saffron steamed rice, page 88). *Nush-e Jan!*

Variation: Chicken can be replaced with 1 pound stew meat (lamb, veal, or beef), cut into 1-inch cubes. In step 1, add 1 cup of water after the tomato juice and simmer for 45 minutes instead of 15 minutes.

Spinach and Prune Khoresh

1½ pounds chicken legs, cut up, with skin and all visible fat removed
2 tablespoons olive oil
3 medium onions, peeled and thinly sliced
1 teaspoon salt
¼ teaspoon freshly ground black pepper

¼ teaspoon turmeric
6 pounds fresh spinach, washed and coarsely chopped, or 2 pounds frozen chopped spinach (3 10-ounce packages)
3 cups pitted prunes
3 tablespoons Seville orange juice, or 4 tablespoons orange juice and 2 tablespoons fresh lime juice

Makes 4 servings
Preparation time: 20 minutes
Cooking time: 2 hours 10 minutes

Khoresh-e esfenaj-o alu

1. Heat a non-stick sauté pan and lightly brown chicken. Add 1 tablespoon oil and 2 of the onions. Fry over medium heat, stirring occasionally, for 20 minutes or until onion becomes translucent. Add salt, pepper, and turmeric. Pour in 1½ cups water, cover and simmer for 15 minutes over low heat.

2. Steam the fresh spinach in a steamer for 10 to 15 minutes. If using frozen spinach, follow package instructions.

3. In a non-stick skillet, brown the remaining onion in 1 tablespoon oil over medium heat, then add the spinach and sauté for another 5 minutes.

4. Add the spinach-and-onion mixture, prunes, and orange juice to the chicken. Cover and simmer 1¼ hours longer over low heat.

5. Check to see that the chicken is cooked. Taste and adjust seasoning. Transfer the stew to a deep casserole. Cover and place in a warm oven until ready to serve.

6. Serve hot from the same dish with *chelow* (saffron steamed rice, page 88). *Nush-e Jan!*

Variation: Chicken can be replaced with 1 pound stew meat (lamb, veal or beef), cut into 1-inch cubes. In step 1, use 2½ cups water instead of 1½ cups, and simmer for 45 minutes instead of 15 minutes.

Pomegranate Khoresh with Chicken or Duck

Makes 4 servings
Preparation time: 30 minutes
Cooking time: 1 hour 40 minutes

Khoresh-e fesenjan ba jujeh ya ordak

1½ pounds chicken legs or duck breast, cut up, with all skin and visible fat removed
2 medium onions, peeled and thinly sliced
1 teaspoon salt
½ pound shelled walnuts, very finely ground in a food processor
1½ cups pomegranate juice or ½ cup pomegranate paste diluted in 1½ cups water
2–3 tablespoons brown sugar

¼ teaspoon ground saffron, dissolved in 1 tablespoon hot water
1 teaspoon ground rose petals
½ teaspoon ground cardamom
¼ teaspoon ground cumin
¼ teaspoon ground cinnamon
2 cups peeled and chopped butternut squash, cut in 1-inch cubes (optional)
2 tablespoons fresh pomegranate seeds (optional)

1. Heat a non-stick sauté pan and lightly brown chicken or duck with onions and salt over medium heat for 10 minutes.

2. Finely grind the walnuts in a food processor. Add the diluted pomegranate paste, brown sugar, saffron water, spices, and butternut squash. Cover and simmer for 1½ hours over low heat, stirring occasionally with a wooden spoon to prevent the nuts from burning.

3. If the sauce is too thick, add warm water to thin it. Taste the sauce and adjust for seasoning and thickness. The stew should be sweet and sour according to your taste. Add pomegranate paste to sour the taste of the sauce or sugar to sweeten it.

4. Transfer the stew from the sauté pan to a deep ovenproof casserole. For decoration, sprinkle with fresh pomegranate seeds and a few walnut pieces. Cover and place in a warm oven until ready to serve.

5. Serve with *chelow* (saffron steamed rice, page 88). *Nush-e Jan!*

Orange Khoresh

Makes 4 servings
Preparation time: 30 minutes
Cooking time: 2 hours

Khoresh-e porteqal

1½ pounds chicken legs, cut up, with skin and all visible fat removed
2 tablespoons olive oil
2 medium onions, peeled and thinly sliced
1 tablespoon flour
2 tablespoons candied orange peel (page 185)
1 teaspoon ground rose petals
½ teaspoon ground cardamom
¼ teaspoon ground cumin
¼ teaspoon ground cinnamon
1 teaspoon salt
¼ teaspoon freshly ground black pepper

1½ cup freshly squeezed orange juice
2 large carrots
4 oranges
2 tablespoons vinegar
¼ cup fresh lime juice
½ cup brown sugar
¼ teaspoon ground saffron, dissolved in 1 tablespoon hot water

Garnish
1 teaspoon slivered pistachios
1 teaspoon slivered almonds

1. Heat a non-stick sauté pan and lightly brown chicken. Add 2 tablespoons oil and the onion. Fry over medium heat, stirring occasionally, for 20 minutes or until onion becomes translucent. Sprinkle in 1 tablespoon flour and mix well.

2. Add candied orange peel, rose petals, cardamom, cumin, cinnamon, salt, and pepper. Pour in the orange juice. Cover and simmer for 35 minutes.

3. Scrape the carrots and slice into thin slivers. Add the carrot to the chicken, cover, and simmer for 1 hour.

4. Peel the oranges, separate them into segments, and peel the membrane from each segment.

5. In a saucepan, combine the vinegar, lime juice, brown sugar, and saffron water. Mix well and simmer for 10 minutes over low heat. Remove from heat, add the orange segments and set aside to macerate for 10 minutes.

6. Transfer the khoresh to a deep ovenproof casserole, carefully arrange the orange segments with the sauce on the top, cover and place in a warm oven until ready to serve.

7. Check to see if the chicken is tender. Taste and adjust seasoning. Add more sugar or lime juice according to your taste.

8. Just before serving, sprinkle the stew with slivered pistachios and almonds. Serve hot from same dish with *chelow* (saffron steamed rice, page 88). *Nush-e Jan!*

Variation: Canned orange segments or tangerines in syrup may be substituted for fresh oranges and sugar.

Rhubarb Khoresh

Makes 4 servings
Preparation time: 30 minutes
Cooking time: 2 hours 10 minutes

خورش ریواس

Khoresh-e rivas

1½ pounds chicken legs, cut up, with skin and all visible fat removed
2 tablespoons olive oil
2 onions, peeled and thinly sliced
1 teaspoon salt
¼ teaspoon freshly ground black pepper
¼ teaspoon turmeric
3 cups chopped fresh parsley

½ cup chopped fresh mint or 2 tablespoons dried
¼ teaspoon ground saffron, dissolved in 1 tablespoon hot water
1 tablespoon tomato paste with no preservatives added
2 tablespoons fresh lime juice
1 pound fresh rhubarb, cut into 1-inch pieces

From ancient times rhubarb has been known for its qualities for cleansing the blood and purifying the system.

1. Heat a non-stick sauté pan and lightly brown chicken. Add 1 tablespoon oil and the onion. Fry over medium heat, stirring occasionally, for 20 minutes or until onion becomes translucent. Add salt, pepper, and turmeric. Pour in 1½ cups water. Cover and simmer for 15 minutes over low heat, stirring occasionally.

2. In a non-stick skillet, fry parsley and mint in 1 tablespoon oil over medium heat, stirring constantly with wooden spoon, for 10 to 15 minutes.

3. Add parsley and mint, saffron water, tomato paste, and lime juice to the chicken. Cover and simmer 55 minutes longer over low heat.

4. Preheat oven to 350°F. Transfer the stew to a deep ovenproof casserole. Arrange the rhubarb on the top and cover the casserole with aluminum foil. Pierce several holes in the foil and place the serving dish in the oven; cook for 25 to 35 minutes or until the rhubarb is tender.

5. Adjust seasoning. If the stew is too sour, add 1 tablespoon sugar. If the rhubarb needs more cooking, continue until done. Remember, rhubarb is fragile; the pieces must be cooked, but not to the point of falling apart.

6. Serve hot from the same dish with *chelow* (saffron steamed rice, page 88). *Nush-e Jan!*

Variation: Chicken can be replaced with 1 pound lean stew meat (lamb, veal, or beef) cut into 1-inch cubes. In step 1, use 2½ cups water instead of 1½ cups and simmer for 1 hour instead of 15 minutes.

Peach Khoresh

Makes 4 servings
Preparation time: 30 minutes
Cooking time: 2 hours

1½ pounds chicken legs, cut up, with skin and all visible fat removed
2 tablespoons olive oil
2 medium onions, peeled and thinly sliced
1 teaspoon salt
¼ teaspoon freshly ground black pepper
1 teaspoon ground rose petals
½ teaspoon ground cardamom
¼ teaspoon ground cumin
¼ teaspoon ground cinnamon
½ cup fresh lime juice
½ cup brown sugar
¼ teaspoon ground saffron, dissolved in 1 tablespoon hot water
5 firm, unripe peaches

Khoresh-e hulu

1. Heat a non-stick sauté pan and lightly brown chicken. Add 1 tablespoon olive oil and onion. Fry over medium heat, stirring occasionally, for 20 minutes or until the onion becomes translucent. Add salt, pepper, rose petals, cardamom, cumin and cinnamon. Pour in 1 cup water. Cover and simmer over low heat for 30 minutes, stirring occasionally.

2. Mix together the lime juice, sugar, and saffron water and stir this mixture into the chicken. Cover and simmer 45 minutes longer over low heat.

3. Wash the peaches well to remove fuzz. Remove pits and cut peaches into ½-inch wedges. Brown in a non-stick skillet in 1 tablespoon oil over medium heat until golden brown. Add the peaches to the sauté pan, cover, and simmer 25 minutes longer.

4. Check to see if chicken and peaches are tender. Taste and adjust seasoning. Transfer the khoresh to a deep ovenproof casserole. Cover and place in a warm oven until ready to serve.

5. Serve hot from the same dish with *chelow* (saffron steamed rice, page 88). *Nush-e Jan!*

Variations:
Chicken can be replaced with 1 pound stew meat (lamb, veal, or beef), cut into 1-inch cubes. In step 1, add 2 cups water in place of 1 cup, and simmer for 1 hour instead of 30 minutes.

3 cups frozen peaches or 3 cups canned sliced peaches in heavy syrup may be substituted for fresh peaches. Just eliminate the sugar and add peaches, without the syrup, in the last 10 minutes of cooking. Alternatively, 2 cups sliced dried peaches may be added to step 1.

Note: Peaches originally came from ancient Persia, and many languages refer to them as Persian fruit. In French, *pêche*; in Russian, *persik*; in Italian, *pesca*; and in German, *pfirsich*.

Quince Khoresh

1½ pounds chicken legs, cut up, with skin and all visible fat removed
2 tablespoons olive oil
2 medium onions, peeled and thinly sliced
1 teaspoon salt
¼ teaspoon freshly ground black pepper
¼ teaspoon ground cinnamon
2 large or 3 small quinces
⅓ cup yellow split peas
¾ cup brown sugar
¼ cup vinegar
¼ cup fresh lime juice
¼ teaspoon ground saffron, dissolved in 1 tablespoon hot water

Makes 4 servings
Preparation time: 20 minutes
Cooking time: 2 hours 20 minutes

خورش به

Khoresh-e beh

Quince is an ancient fruit originally from Persia and is used in Persian cooking.

1. Heat a non-stick sauté pan and lightly brown chicken. Add 1 tablespoon olive oil and the onion. Fry over medium heat, stirring occasionally, for 20 minutes or until the onion becomes translucent. Add salt, pepper, and cinnamon. Stir in 1½ cups water. Cover and simmer for 30 minutes over low heat, stirring occasionally.

2. Wash but do not peel the quinces. Core using an apple corer, cut into quarters, and remove seeds; cut into wedges.

3. Brown quince in 1 tablespoon oil in a non-stick skillet for about 10 to 15 minutes, until golden brown. Add it to the chicken. Cover and simmer 30 minutes.

4. Add the yellow split peas, brown sugar, vinegar, lime juice and saffron water. Cover and simmer for 30 to 45 minutes over low heat. (The cooking time depends on the type of yellow split peas used.)

5. Taste the khoresh and adjust seasoning by adding more sugar or lime juice. Transfer to a deep ovenproof casserole. Cover and place in a warm oven.

6. Serve hot in the same dish with *chelow* (saffron steamed rice, page 88).
Nush-e Jan!

Note: If using American yellow split peas, cover and simmer for only 20 minutes in step 4, since American peas cook faster.

Variation: Chicken can be replaced with 1 pound stew meat (lamb, veal, or beef), cut into 1-inch cubes. In step 1, add 3 cups water in place of 1½ cups and simmer for 1 hour instead of 30 minutes.

Apple Khoresh

1½ pounds chicken legs, cut up, with skin and all visible fat removed
2 tablespoons olive oil
2 medium onions, peeled and thinly sliced
1 teaspoon salt
¼ teaspoon pepper

½ teaspoon ground cinnamon
1 cup apple juice
1 tablespoon lime juice
3 tablespoons brown sugar
½ teaspoon ground saffron, dissolved in 2 tablespoons hot water
5 tart cooking apples
1 cup pitted dried tart cherries

Makes 4 servings
Preparation time: 20 minutes
Cooking time: 2 hours

Khoresh-e sib

1. Heat a non-stick sauté pan and lightly brown chicken. Add 1 tablespoon olive oil and the onion. Fry over medium heat, stirring occasionally, for 20 minutes or until the onion becomes translucent. Season with salt, pepper, and cinnamon. Add apple and lime juices. Cover and simmer for 30 minutes over low heat, stirring occasionally.

2. Add brown sugar and saffron water. Cover and simmer 30 minutes longer.

3. Peel and core the apples and cut into wedges. Brown in 1 tablespoon oil in a non-stick skillet over medium heat for 10 to 15 minutes, until golden brown.

4. Taste the khoresh and correct seasoning. Add either more sugar or lime juice if necessary. The sauce should taste sweet and sour.

5. Preheat oven to 350°F. Transfer the stew to a deep ovenproof casserole. Arrange the apples and cherries on the top. Cover and bake for 30 to 40 minutes longer. Serve from the same dish with *chelow* (saffron steamed rice, page 88). *Nush-e Jan!*

Variation: You may substitute the dried cherries with ⅓ cup yellow split peas cooked in 2 cups of water for 20 minutes, drained, and added in step 5.

Fresh Herb Khoresh

Makes 4 servings
Preparation time: 25 minutes
Cooking time: 4 hours

خورش قورمه سبزی

Khoresh-e qormeh sabzi

Note: If you must use dried herbs, reduce the measurement to ¼ of the fresh herbs. Place the dried herbs in a sieve in a bowl of lukewarm water and allow to soak for 15 minutes. Remove the sieve and use the herbs as per the recipe.

2 pounds lamb shanks
2 tablespoons olive oil
2 medium onions, peeled and thinly sliced
2 cloves garlic
1½ teaspoons salt
¼ teaspoon freshly ground black pepper
1 teaspoon turmeric
½ teaspoon ground saffron, dissolved in 1 tablespoon hot water
½ cup dried kidney beans
4 whole dried Persian limes (*limu-omani*), pierced

4 cups finely chopped fresh parsley
1 cup finely chopped garlic chives or scallions
1 cup finely chopped fresh coriander
1 cup chopped fresh fenugreek leaves or 4 tablespoons dried fenugreek sprinkled with warm water
2 tablespoons dried Persian lime powder (*limu-omani*) or 4 tablespoons fresh lime juice

1. Place lamb shank in a large pot, cover with cold water, bring to a boil, and then drain and remove all excess fat. Heat a non-stick sauté pan and lightly brown the shanks. Add 1 tablespoon olive oil, the onions and garlic and fry, stirring occasionally, for 20 minutes over medium heat. Add salt, pepper, turmeric, saffron water, kidney beans and whole dried Persian limes; sauté lightly for a few minutes longer. Pour in 4 to 4½ cups water. Bring to a boil, cover and simmer over low heat, stirring occasionally.

2. Meanwhile, fry the chopped parsley, garlic chives or scallions, coriander, and fenugreek in a non-stick skillet over medium heat for 10 minutes. Add 1 tablespoon oil and continue frying another 10 minutes, stirring constantly with a wooden spoon or until the aroma of frying herbs rises (this stage is very important to the taste of the stew).

3. Add the sautéed herbs and lime powder or lime juice to the khoresh. Cover and simmer for 2½ to 3 hours over low heat, stirring occasionally.

4. Check to see if meat and kidney beans are tender. Taste the stew and adjust seasoning. Transfer to a deep casserole; cover and place in a warm oven until ready to serve.

5. Serve hot from the same dish with *chelow* (saffron steamed rice, page 88). *Nush-e Jan!*

Eggplant Khoresh

Makes 4 servings
Preparation time: 20 minutes
Cooking time: 2 hours 15 minutes

1½ pounds chicken legs, with skin and all visible fat removed, cut up
2 tablespoons olive oil
2 medium onions, peeled and thinly sliced
2 cloves of garlic, peeled and crushed
1 teaspoon salt
¼ teaspoon freshly ground black pepper
1 teaspoon turmeric
1 teaspoon ground saffron, dissolved in 4 tablespoons hot water
2 cups fresh squeezed tomato juice
1 cup unripe grapes (*ghureh*)
4 tablespoons lime juice
3 medium or 9 slim eggplants
2 egg whites, lightly beaten

Garnish
1 large onion, peeled and thinly sliced
1 tablespoon olive oil
1 large tomato, peeled and left whole

That food which I most cherish is the sour-grape, chicken, and eggplant dish.

آن غذائی که مرا چون جان است   غوره و جوجه و بادمجان است

خورش بادمجان

Khoresh-e bademjan

Note: Unripe grapes (*ghureh*) are important to the taste of this khoresh and are available in cans at Persian specialty stores. However, if you do not have any they can be replaced with 4 more tablespoons of lime juice.

1. Heat a non-stick sauté pan and lightly brown chicken. Add 1 tablespoon olive oil, the onion, and the garlic. Fry over medium heat, stirring occasionally, for 20 minutes or until the onion becomes translucent. Add salt, pepper, turmeric, and saffron water.

2. Pour in 2 cups tomato juice, unripe grapes, and lime juice. Cover and simmer over low heat for 30 minutes.

3. Peel eggplants and cut lengthwise in quarters if they are large. Place in a colander, sprinkle both sides with water and 1 tablespoon salt, and set aside for 20 minutes to remove the bitter taste (disgorging). Rinse and pat dry.

4. Brush each side of the eggplant with egg white to reduce the oil needed for frying. In a non-stick skillet, fry the eggplant in 1 tablespoon oil over medium heat until golden brown.

5. For the garnish, lightly brown the onion in a non-stick skillet in 1 tablespoon oil over medium heat; set aside. In the same skillet, sauté the whole tomato.

6. Preheat the oven to 350°F. Transfer the chicken and sauce into a deep oven-proof casserole; arrange the eggplant, then onion and tomato, on the top. Cover and bake for 45 minutes, then remove cover and bake another 15 minutes.

7. Adjust seasoning and serve immediately from the same dish or keep warm in the oven until ready to serve. Serve with *chelow* (saffron steamed rice, page 88). *Nush-e Jan!*

Potato Khoresh

Makes 4 servings
Preparation time: 20 minutes
Cooking time: 2 hours 15 minutes

خورش قیمه

Khoresh-e qeymeh

2 onions, peeled and thinly sliced
1½ pounds stew meat (lamb, veal, or beef) cut into ½-inch pieces
4 tablespoons olive oil
4 whole dried Persian limes (*limu-omani*), pierced
1 teaspoon salt
¼ teaspoon freshly ground black pepper
½ teaspoon turmeric
1 teaspoon ground saffron, dissolved in 4 tablespoons hot water

2 cups fresh squeezed tomato juice
1 teaspoon ground rose petals
½ teaspoon ground cardamom
¼ teaspoon ground cumin
¼ teaspoon ground cinnamon
1 tablespoon candied orange peel (page 185)
2 tablespoons lime juice
⅓ cup yellow split peas
1 pound or 2 large potatoes, peeled and cut into sticks

1. In a non-stick sauté pan, brown the onions and meat in 2 tablespoons oil over medium heat, stirring occasionally, for 30 minutes. Add dried Persian limes, salt, pepper, turmeric, and saffron water. Sauté for 2 minutes longer. Pour in tomato juice and 2 cups water and bring to a boil. Cover and simmer over low heat for 55 minutes, stirring occasionally.

2. Add rose petals, cardamom, cumin, and cinnamon, candied orange peel, and lime juice. Cover and simmer another 45 minutes.

3. Add yellow split peas, cover and simmer for 30 to 45 minutes or until tender.

4. During this time fry the potato sticks. Place the potato sticks in a large plastic bag. Add 2 tablespoons olive oil, seal the bag, and shake well to cover potatoes with oil. Transfer potatoes to a heated non-stick skillet, then fry for about 15 to 20 minutes over medium heat, stirring occasionally with a wooden spoon. Remove from heat and set aside.

5. Check to see if meat and peas are tender. Taste the stew and adjust seasoning. Transfer to a deep casserole, cover and place in a warm oven until ready to serve.

6. Just before serving, arrange the french fries on top of the khoresh. Serve with *chelow* (saffron steamed rice, page 88), *torshi* (Persian pickles) and fresh vegetables and herbs (*sabzi-khordan*) on the side. *Nush-e Jan!*

Yogurt Khoresh

2 onions, peeled and thinly sliced
1½ pounds chicken legs, with
    skin and all visible fat removed,
    cut up
¾ cup chopped celery (2 stalks)
1 tablespoon olive oil
1 teaspoon salt
¼ teaspoon freshly ground
    black pepper

2 tablespoons curry powder
1 tablespoon flour
2 tablespoons lime juice
2 cups low-fat yogurt

Garnish
¼ cup slivered almonds
¼ cup raisins

Makes 4 servings
Preparation time: 15 minutes
Cooking time: 1 hour 40 minutes

Khoresh-e mast

1. In a non-stick sauté pan, fry onions with the chicken and celery in 1 tablespoon oil over medium heat for 10 minutes. Sprinkle with salt, pepper, curry powder, and flour. Mix well. Do not add water since the chicken will produce its own juice. Add lime juice, cover, and simmer for about 1 hour 30 minutes over low heat, stirring occasionally.

2. In a bowl, beat the yogurt well with a fork.

3. When the chicken is cooked, just before serving, stir in the yogurt and simmer for 5 minutes over low heat, occasionally stirring gently (do not boil the yogurt).

4. Check to see if the chicken is tender. Taste and adjust seasoning. Transfer the stew to a deep serving dish.

5. Garnish with almonds and raisins and serve hot with *chelow* (saffron steamed rice, page 88). *Nush-e Jan!*

Variation: Curry powder and celery may be replaced with 1 teaspoon saffron dissolved in 4 tablespoons hot water and ½ cup candied orange peel (page 185) in this recipe. Add the candied orange peel in step 1; mix the saffron with the yogurt in step 2.

Fruit Chutney

Makes about 4 pints
Preparation and cooking time:
4 hours
Curing time: 10 days

تُرشیِ مِیوہ

Torshi-e miveh

*Note: If you are using dried tamarind, cover the fruit with vinegar, bring to a boil and simmer over medium heat for 15 minutes, then drain in a colander set over a bowl. Using the back of a spoon, press the tamarind to remove the seeds, threads, and pods. For the best results both for flavor and for your budget, buy fruit as it comes into season. Wash, prepare, and cook with vinegar as in step 2, then store in airtight containers in a cool place. At the end of the year (or when you have collected and prepared much or all the fruit), place all the fruit in a large saucepan, add the spices, and continue from step 3. The fresher your fruit when prepared, the better your *torshi!*

Persian Chutney Spice Mixture
  (*Advieh-ye Torshi*)
2 teaspoons ground green cumin
1 teaspoon ground black cumin
3 teaspoons ground angelica
  powder (*gol-par*)
½ teaspoon freshly ground
  black pepper
½ teaspoon ground turmeric
3 teaspoons ground coriander seeds
2 teaspoons ground cinnamon
3 teaspoons ground ginger
1 teaspoon ground cardamom
1 tablespoon powdered dried
  Persian lime (*limu-omani*)

Fruit and Vegetables
1 pound apricots, chopped
½ pound fresh or dried tamarind*
2 pounds pitted dates, chopped, or 1
  cup honey or sugar
1 pound dried pitted prunes,
  finely chopped
1 pound seedless grapes,
  finely chopped

1 pound apples, cored
  and finely chopped
1 pound quinces, cored
  and finely chopped
1 pound persimmons,
  finely chopped
1 pound pitted sour cherries
2 red peppers, seeds removed and
  finely chopped
2 navel oranges, peeled, seeds
  removed and finely chopped
5 pounds peaches, peeled, pitted
  and finely chopped
1 bulb of fresh garlic, peeled
  and crushed
5 pounds mangoes, peeled
  and chopped
2 or more quarts apple vinegar

Seasoning
2 teaspoons ground saffron
2 tablespoons nigella seeds
  (*siah daneh*)
2 tablespoons salt

A food processor can be used to chop the fruit and vegetables.

1. Prepare the Persian chutney spice mixture (*advieh-ye torshi*) by placing all the ground spice ingredients in a bowl and mixing well. Set aside.

2. Place all the prepared fruit and vegetables in a large pot. Cover with the vinegar and simmer for 2 to 3 hours over low heat, stirring occasionally with a wooden spoon.

3. Remove the pot from heat. Add the Persian chutney spice mixture and the seasoning to the pot and mix well. Adjust seasoning to taste; add more vinegar if too dry.

4. Sterilize canning jars in boiling water. Drain and dry thoroughly. Fill the jars to within ½ inch of the top with chutney, then end with a splash of vinegar and a bit of salt on top. Seal the jars.

5. Store the jars for at least 10 days in a cool, dark place before using. The result should be a healthful, sweet-and-sour chutney. *Nush-e Jan!*

Pickled Garlic

1 pound garlic bulbs
½ cup dried barberries, cleaned,
    soaked for 20 minutes in cold
    water, and drained
1 quart or more vinegar

Makes 2 pints
Preparation time: 20 minutes
Curing time: 6 weeks

Torshi-e sir

1. Peel off just 1 outside layer of the garlic bulbs.

2. Fill in the center of each bulb with 1 teaspoon barberries.

3. Sterilize canning jars in boiling water and dry thoroughly.

4. Fill the jars nearly to top with garlic bulbs. Fill the jar to within ½ inch of the top with vinegar. Add a bit of salt to the top. Seal the jars.

5. Store the jars in a cool, dark place for at least 6 weeks before using. Garlic pickle is at its best when 7 years old, when it will be sweet, like a preserve. *Nush-e Jan!*

Eggplant Pickle

20 small pickling eggplants (Italian)
1¼ quarts wine vinegar
2 tablespoons salt
2 cups chopped fresh mint
1 cup chopped fresh coriander or
     parsley
½ pound or 3 bulbs of garlic, sepa-
     rated into cloves, peeled, and
     finely chopped

Makes 2 pints
Preparation and cooking
time: 40 minutes
Curing time: 40 days

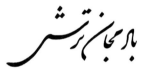

Bademjan torshi

1. Wash the eggplants and remove the stems. Make a lengthwise slit on 1 side of each eggplant.

2. Place the eggplants in a laminated pot, cover with vinegar, bring to a boil and simmer over medium heat for 20 minutes, or until tender.

3. Drain the eggplant and let stand for a few hours until completely dry. In a saucepan, bring to a boil 2 tablespoons salt and 1 quart vinegar.

4. Mix 1 tablespoon salt, herbs, and garlic together. Stuff each of the eggplants with the herb mixture and press shut.

5. Sterilize the canning jars in boiling water. Drain and dry thoroughly. Fill them to within ½ inch of the top with stuffed eggplants. Cover with salted vinegar. Seal the jars.

6. Store the jars in a cool, dark place for at least 40 days before using. *Nush-e Jan!*

Note: Autumn eggplants make excellent pickles.

Golden Plum Preserves

2 pounds golden plums
4 cups brown sugar
1 cup water
2 tablespoons lime juice
1 teaspoon ground cardamom or
    ¼ cup rose water (optional)

Makes 4 half-pint jars
Preparation time: 15 minutes
plus overnight macerating
Cooking time: 45 minutes

Moraba-ye alu zard

1. Do not remove stems from the plums; wash and peel them. (To peel plums more quickly, blanch them first for 1 minute in boiling water—the skin will come off easily.)

2. Place brown sugar and plums in a large saucepan. Macerate overnight. Remove the plums from the sugar. Add 1 cup water, bring to a boil, reduce heat and let simmer over medium heat for 10 minutes.

3. Add the plums and lime juice. Simmer uncovered for 30 to 35 minutes over medium heat, or until the syrup has thickened enough to coat the back of a spoon, stirring gently from time to time. Add cardamom or rose water.

4. Sterilize jelly jars in boiling water. Drain and dry thoroughly. Fill the jars with jam and seal them tightly. Store in a cool, dark place. *Nush-e Jan!*

Quince Preserves

2 pounds quince (about 3 medium
    quinces)
1½ cups water
4 cups sugar
¼ teaspoon vanilla extract or 1
    vanilla bean, or 1 stick cinnamon
4 tablespoons fresh lime juice

Makes 4 half-pint jars
Preparation time: 25 minutes
Cooking time: 2 hours 45
minutes

Moraba-ye beh

1. Quarter the quinces and remove the cores. Slice the quarters into wedges. Place in a container full of cold water and a splash of vinegar to prevent the quince from turning black. Wash and drain.

2. Place quince wedges and 1½ cups water in a pot. Bring to a boil over high heat, then reduce heat, cover and let simmer over low heat for 15 minutes. Add the sugar and vanilla extract. Place a clean dish towel or 2 layers of paper towel over the pot and cover firmly with lid. Let simmer over low heat for 1 hour.

3. Add lime juice. Cover and simmer for 1¼ to 1½ hours more over low heat, stirring gently from time to time, until the syrup has thickened and the quince has turned red. Remove from heat and allow to cool.

4. Sterilize jelly jars in boiling water, drain and let dry. Fill the jars with hot preserves and seal. Store in a cool, dark place. *Nush-e Jan!*

Rose Petal Preserves

1 pound fresh rose petals, or
  2 ounces (60 grams) dried rose
  petals
2 cups sugar
1½ cups water
¼ tablespoon lime juice
1 cup slivered pistachios
2 tablespoons rose water (if using
  dried rose petals)

Makes 1 half-pint jar
Preparation time: 35 minutes
Cooking time: 40 minutes

Moraba-ye gol-e Mohammadi

1. Select fresh pink rose petals. Cut off the white ends of the petals and wash carefully. Place rose petals in a saucepan and cover with cool water. Let stand for 15 minutes. If using dried rose petals, place in a pot, cover with water and bring to a boil. Drain in a colander, rinse with cold water and let dry. Toast the rose petals in a skillet for a few minutes over low heat.

2. Place sugar and water in a laminated pot. Bring to a boil, reduce the heat, and let simmer over medium heat for 20 minutes, or until the syrup has thickened. Add lime juice, rose petals, slivered pistachios, and rose water, mix well and simmer over medium heat for 10 minutes longer. Remove from heat.

3. Sterilize jelly jars in boiling water; drain and let dry. Fill the jars with the hot jelly and seal. Store in a cool, dark place. *Nush-e Jan!*

Orange Blossom Preserves

1 pound fresh or 2 ounces (60 grams) dried orange blossoms
2 cups sugar
1½ cups water
1 tablespoon orange blossom water (if using dried blossoms)
2 tablespoons fresh lime juice

Makes 1 half-pint jar
Preparation time: 35 minutes
plus 1 day's marination
Cooking time: 45 minutes

مربای هب کـ نارنج

Moraba-ye bahar narenj

1. Carefully wash the orange blossoms, separate the petals, and soak in a bowl of cold water. Set in refrigerator for a day, changing the water several times.

2. Bring 4 cups of water to a boil in a laminated pan over high heat. Add the blossoms, reduce heat and simmer for 10 minutes; drain in a colander and rinse with cold water. This step is essential to remove any traces of bitterness.

3. In a heavy saucepan, bring the sugar and water to a boil, then reduce heat and simmer for 15 to 20 minutes over medium heat. Add orange blossom petals (if using dried blossoms, add 1 tablespoon orange blossom water), add lime juice and simmer 15 minutes longer until the syrup has thickened enough to coat the back of a spoon. Remove pan from heat.

4. Sterilize jelly jars in boiling water; drain and let dry. Fill the jars with the hot preserves and seal. Store in a cool, dark place. *Nush-e Jan!*

Almond Cookies

1 pound blanched almonds
5 egg whites
1½ cups confectioners' sugar
½ teaspoon ground cardamom or
   2 tablespoons rose water
2 tablespoons unsalted slivered
   pistachios or toasted almond
   slices for decoration

Makes 20 pieces
Preparation time: 40 minutes
Cooking time: 10 to 15 minutes

Nan-e badami

1. In a food processor, grind blanched almonds to produce almond powder.

2. In a mixing bowl, beat the egg whites until foamy. Slowly mix in sugar, almond powder, and cardamom or rose water. Gently mix until a dough is formed.

3. Preheat oven to 350°F. Grease a cookie sheet.

4. Scoop out a full tablespoon of the dough and place it on the greased cookie sheet. Continue, leaving 2½ inches between each piece for expansion. Decorate each piece with a few slivered pistachios or toasted almond slices.

5. Place the cookie sheet in the center of the oven and bake for 10 to 20 minutes, until the cookies are golden.

6. Remove the cookies from the oven, allow to cool and then remove them from the cookie sheet. Keep them in a cookie jar.

7. When ready to serve, arrange in a pyramid on a footed cake dish. *Nush-e Jan!*

Honey Almond Brittle

1 cup sugar
3 tablespoons pure honey
4 tablespoons corn oil
1½ cups unsalted slivered blanched almonds
½ teaspoon ground saffron, dissolved in 2 tablespoons of rose water

4 tablespoons unsalted chopped pistachios for decoration

Makes 25 pieces
Preparation time: 15 minutes
Cooking time: 10 minutes

سهان عسل

Sohan asal

1. In a heavy saucepan over high heat, melt the sugar and honey with oil for 5 minutes, stirring occasionally.

2. Add the slivered almonds to the mixture. Stir from time to time, for about 3 to 5 minutes, until the mixture is firm and golden.

3. Add the saffron-rose water mixture and cook for another 2 to 4 minutes, stirring occasionally, until the mixture is a golden brown color. Be careful: it should not be dark brown. Place a bowl of ice water next to the stove. Drop a spoonful of the hot almond mixture into the water: If it hardens immediately, the mixture is ready. Reduce the heat to very low.

4. Spread a piece of wax paper on a flat surface. Place teaspoonfuls of the mixture on wax paper, leaving a 1-inch space between each. Garnish immediately with the chopped pistachios.

5. Allow the almonds to cool, then remove them from the paper.

6. Arrange on a serving platter. Cover with a sheet of aluminum foil to keep them crisp or keep in an airtight container or cookie jar. *Nush-e Jan!*

Baklava

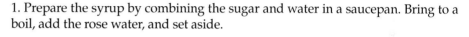

Syrup
2½ cups sugar
1½ cups water
½ cup rose water

Filling
2 pounds of blanched almonds,
  ground
2 cups sugar
2 tablespoons ground cardamom

Dough
¼ cup low-fat milk, 2% milk fat
½ cup corn oil
1 tablespoon syrup (prepared)
¼ cup rose water
1 egg
2 cups sifted all-purpose flour
6 tablespoons corn oil for baking
2 tablespoons chopped or ground
  pistachios for garnish

Makes 1 full sheet
Preparation time: 35 minutes
plus 1 hour for dough to rise

Baqlava

1. Prepare the syrup by combining the sugar and water in a saucepan. Bring to a boil, add the rose water, and set aside.

2. For the filling, finely grind the almonds, sugar, and cardamom together in a food processor. Set aside.

3. For the dough, combine the milk, corn oil, syrup, rose water, and egg in a food processor or dough maker. Add the flour and mix well for 5 to 10 minutes to form a dough that does not stick to your hands. Divide the dough into 2 balls of equal size and place in a bowl. Cover with a clean towel and let rest for 30 minutes.

4. When the dough has risen, grease a 17-by-11-by-1-inch sheet with ¼ cup oil and preheat the oven to 350°F.

5. Prepare a large, wide area for rolling out the dough. Cover the surface with a dusting of flour. Remove 1 ball of dough from the bowl and roll out into a very thin rectangular layer with a thin wooden rolling pin (the rolled dough should be thinner than a pie crust). Roll dough from the center to the outside edge in all directions, giving it a quarter turn occasionally for an even thickness. The finished dough should be able to overlap the cookie sheet.

6. Roll the thin layer of dough around the wooden rolling pin. Place it on the greased cookie sheet and unroll the dough until it covers the whole cookie sheet. Do not cut off the excess dough; let the dough hang over the edge of the cookie sheet 1 inch on all sides.

7. Evenly sprinkle all the almond-filling mixture on top of the dough. Spread, smooth, and press down the mixture on the dough with your hand.

8. Roll the second ball of dough out into a very thin rectangular layer as in step 5. Roll the layer around the rolling pin, place on top of the filling mixture in the cookie sheet, and unroll the dough to cover the mixture, allowing it to hang over all sides like the bottom layer. Press down on the dough evenly with your hands all over the dough's surface.

9. Trace an outline of 1-inch diamond shapes on the top layer with a sharp knife. Guide the knife in a straight line, assuring that each piece will eventually be of equal size. Press down on the dough evenly with your hand.

10. Fold and roll the overhanging dough from the top layer under the dough from the bottom layer. Press together and pinch the top and bottom edges together to seal like a pie, forming a rim around the edge of the cookie sheet.

11. Using a sharp knife, hold down the dough with 1 hand while cutting it into diamond shapes with the other. With a brush, paint the dough with 2 tablespoons oil all over and place the baking pan in the middle of the preheated oven.

12. Bake for 10 to 15 minutes (depending on your oven). When the baklava is pink, remove it from the oven and pour half of the syrup all over the top.

13. Decorate the baklava with chopped or ground pistachio nuts. Cover it tightly with aluminum foil and let stand for 24 hours until it settles.

14. Using a sharp knife, lift the diamond pieces out of the baking pan and carefully arrange on a serving dish, or serve from the same dish.

15. Keep this pastry covered, in the refrigerator or freezer. *Nush-e Jan!*

Lavash Bread

1 package or 1 tablespoon dry yeast
2½ cups warm water
4–5 cups sifted all-purpose flour
1 teaspoon salt
1 teaspoon sugar
Oil for handling dough
1 tablespoon poppy or sesame seed

Baking stone
Baker's peel

Makes 6–8 small loaves
Preparation time: 40 minutes
plus 1 hour's rising time
Cooking time: 3 to 4 minutes
per loaf

Nan-e lavash

1. In a mixing bowl, dissolve the yeast in 1 cup warm water; add 1 tablespoon flour and 1 teaspoon salt. Allow to ferment for 10 minutes at room temperature.

2. Use the dough hook on an electric mixer and beat for 20 to 25 minutes, gradually adding the rest of the water. When the dough is beaten, its ability to absorb water increases. Add sugar. Gradually add sifted flour, stirring constantly at low speed for 20 more minutes. Cover bowl with a clean towel and allow dough to rise for a few minutes at room temperature.

3. Place a baking stone on the lower shelf of your oven; preheat oven to 500°F.

4. Working on an oiled surface, knead the dough for a few minutes with oiled hands. Divide it into balls the size of apples. Place a ball on a lightly oiled surface or wooden board and use a thin, oiled rolling pin to roll it out as thin as possible, to about 10 inches in diameter. Take the dough and flip it across the back of your hand to stretch it a little. Repeat this process for each ball of dough.

5. Lightly flour the baker's peel. Transfer the dough to the far end of the peel and sprinkle it with poppy or sesame seeds. Open oven door and quickly slide dough onto the hot baking stone. Close oven door and bake the dough in the lower level for 3 to 4 minutes. Remove from the oven. Cook each loaf individually and continue until all loaves have been baked. Wrap the *lavash* bread loaves in a clean towel and set aside for 10 minutes while the towel absorbs excess moisture; remove the towel and serve the bread hot. Otherwise, wrap the bread in aluminum foil or a clean cloth, or place it in a plastic bag. *Nush-e Jan!*

Saffron Pudding

1 cup rice
8–10 cups water
3½ cups sugar
¼ cup corn oil
½ cup unsalted slivered almonds
½ teaspoon ground saffron, dissolved in 2 tablespoons hot water

1 teaspoon ground cardamom
½ cup rose water

Garnish
2 teaspoons ground cinnamon
2 teaspoons slivered almonds
2 teaspoons slivered pistachios

Makes 8 servings
Preparation time: 5 minutes
Cooking time: 1 hour 40 minutes

Sholeh zard

1. Pick over and wash rice, changing the water several times.

2. Combine the rice with 8 cups of water in a large pot and bring to a boil, skimming the foam as it rises. Cover and simmer for 35 minutes over medium heat until the rice is quite soft.

3. Add 2 more cups of warm water; add sugar and simmer for 25 minutes longer, stirring occasionally (do not stir too much). Add the corn oil, almonds, saffron water, cardamom, and rose water. Mix well. Cover and simmer over low heat for 20 minutes; remove cover and simmer over low heat for another 20 minutes or until the mixture has thickened to a pudding. Remove from heat.

4. Immediately spoon the pudding into individual serving dishes or a large bowl. Decorate with cinnamon, almonds, and pistachios. Chill in the refrigerator.

5. Serve the pudding cold. *Nush-e Jan!*

Paradise Custard

¾ cup cornstarch, wheat starch, or
    rice starch (rice flour)
4 cups low-fat milk (2% milk fat)
1 cup sugar
10 cardamom pods, peeled
¼ cup rose water

Garnish
⅓ cup slivered almonds, toasted, or
    1 teaspoon ground pistachios

Makes 6 servings
Preparation time: 10 minutes
plus 2 hours' setting time
Cooking time: 15 minutes

Yakh dar behesht

1. In a saucepan, dissolve the cornstarch in milk and add the sugar. Cook over medium heat for about 5 minutes, stirring constantly until the mixture has thickened.

2. Add the cardamom pods and rose water. Cook for a few minutes, stirring constantly to prevent sticking and lumping, until the mixture reaches the consistency of a pudding. Remove saucepan from heat.

3. Immediately transfer the custard to a serving dish. Decorate with toasted almonds or pistachios.

4. Chill the custard in the refrigerator for 2 hours and serve it cold. *Nush-e Jan!*

Pomegranate Jello

3 envelopes unflavored gelatin
5 cups freshly squeezed
     pomegranate juice
2 tablespoons lime juice
2 tablespoons sugar
     (if pomegranates are too sour)
Seeds of 4 fresh pomegranates
2 tablespoons slivered pistachios

Makes 6 servings
Preparation time: 15 minutes
Setting time: 8 hours

Jeleh-ye anar

1. In a large bowl, sprinkle the unflavored gelatin over 1 cup of cold pomegranate juice. Let stand for 1 minute.

2. In a saucepan, warm 4 cups of pomegranate juice and 2 tablespoons lime juice.

3. Add the softened gelatin to the saucepan. Stir constantly for 5 minutes, until gelatin is completely dissolved.

4. Taste it. If too sour, add sugar to taste. Pour the mixture into a mold or a bowl. Let it cool.

5. Scatter the pomegranate seeds on top of the mixture. Chill it in the refrigerator until firm.

6. Serve pomegranate jello with yogurt or ice cream sprinkled with pomegranate seeds or slivered pistachios. *Nush-e Jan!*

Variation: This jello can be equally well made with tart cherries or rhubarb. Replace the pomegranate juice and seeds with tart cherry juice and tart cherries or with rhubarb juice.

Quince Custard

6 pounds quinces or 8 medium quinces
3 cups water
2 cups sugar
2 tablespoons quince seeds wrapped in a cheesecloth, tied in a knot
10 cardamom pods, peeled
1 cup ground pistachios for garnish

Makes 6 servings
Preparation time: 15 minutes
Cooking time: 2 hours

لوزِبه

Loz-e beh

This dish is often associated with the Winter Festival, Shab-e Yalda.

1. Wash and core the quinces, cut into wedges and place in a pot. Cover with 3 cups of water, add ¼ cup sugar and the wrapped quince seeds, and bring to a boil. Reduce heat, cover and simmer over low heat for about 1½ hours or until tender, stirring occasionally.

2. Remove the quince seeds from the pot and discard them. Puree the quince in a food processor and return to the pot. Add remaining sugar and cardamom pods. Cover and simmer over low heat for 35 minutes, stirring occasionally with a wooden spoon, or until all the water has evaporated.

3. Transfer the quince custard to a flat serving platter. Pack it firmly with a spoon and garnish with ground pistachios. Cover firmly, chill the custard in the refrigerator, then serve as a dessert. *Nush-e Jan!*

Cantaloupe and Peach Sherbet

2 large fresh peaches or 1 16-ounce
  can sliced peaches in heavy syrup
1 cantaloupe or honeydew melon
2 tablespoons sugar (if using fresh
  peaches)
1 tablespoon fresh lime juice
2 tablespoons rose water or orange
  blossom water
5 fresh mint leaves

Makes 4 servings
Preparation time: 15 minutes
plus 30 minutes to chill

كمپوت هلو و طالبی

Sherbet-e hulu va talebi

1. Peel and slice the peaches.

2. Peel and slice the cantaloupe or melon into small 1-inch pieces. Use a melon baller if you have one.

3. In individual serving bowls, combine sugar, lime juice, and rose or orange blossom water; add the sliced melon and peaches. Stir gently. Cover and chill in the refrigerator.

4. Adjust to taste by adding more sugar if necessary. Decorate with mint leaves and serve immediately. *Nush-e Jan!*

Variation: You may puree and combine all the ingredients in a food processor and chill in the refrigerator, or make *Paloodeh-ye Garmak*—puree the cantaloupe with sugar and 3 ice cubes in a food processor. Add a few drops of rose water, and decorate with mint leaves and rose petals. This dessert can also be garnished with rice stick sherbet (page 179).

Rice Stick Sherbet

Makes 4 servings
Preparation time: 15 minutes
Cooking time: 1 minute
Setting time: 24 hours

فالوده شیرازی

Paludeh

Sherbet
1 ounce (30 grams) thin rice noodles
  or Chinese rice sticks, broken
  into 2-inch pieces
1 cup sugar
1 cup water
3 tablespoons rose water
2 tablespoons fresh lime juice

Garnish
2 tablespoons slivered pistachios
2 tablespoons dried tart cherries
4 tablespoons fresh-squeezed lime
  juice (optional)

1. Place the rice noodles in a bowl. Cover with cold water, soak for 30 minutes and drain.

2. In a pot, bring 8 cups of water to a boil.

3. Add the rice noodles and boil for 20 seconds. Drain, run cold water through the noodles, and set aside.

4. Place sugar and water in a saucepan and bring to a boil over medium heat. Remove the pan from the heat immediately. Add rose water and lime juice and allow to cool.

5. Pour the mixture into an ice cream machine bowl. Add half of the rice noodles. Cover and turn on the ice cream machine for 35 minutes.

6. Stop the machine and add the rest of the noodles. Turn machine on for an additional 25 minutes.

7. Remove sherbet and spoon into individual serving bowls. Garnish with pistachios, tart cherries and lime juice. *Nush-e Jan!*

Note: This sherbet can also be served with sliced fresh melon or garnished with rose petals.

Quince-Lime Syrup

2 pounds quinces (about 2 cups juice)
4 cups brown sugar
2 cups water
½ cup fresh lime juice

Makes 1 pint
Preparation time: 10 minutes
Cooking time: 55 minutes

شربت به لیمو

Sharbat-e beh limu

1. Quarter the quinces and remove cores with a knife. Do not peel. Wash and pat dry, and process in a juicer.

2. Bring the brown sugar and water to a boil in a saucepan. Add the quince juice and boil for 30 minutes over medium heat, stirring occasionally; add the lime juice and cook for another 15 minutes or until the syrup thickens.

3. Remove the saucepan from heat. Allow to cool. Pour the syrup into a clean, dry bottle and cork tightly.

4. In a pitcher, mix 1 part syrup, 3 parts water, and 2 ice cubes per person. Stir with a spoon. *Nush-e-Jan!*

Variation: Another way to make this syrup is to tie up the cleaned, sliced, and washed quince in cheesecloth. Cover and cook in a pot with 4 cups water for 1 hour and 30 minutes over medium heat, until the quince is tender. Squeeze and remove the cheesecloth and its contents, add 2 cups sugar, 2 cups water, and ½ cup fresh lime juice to the pot; cover and cook over medium heat for another 30 minutes. Continue with step 3 above.

Seville Orange Syrup

5–6 pounds Seville oranges (2 cups
  Seville orange juice)
4 cups brown sugar
2 cups water

Garnish
Fresh orange leaves
Orange blossoms

Makes 2 pints
Preparation time: 5 minutes
Cooking time: 35 minutes

Sharbat-e narenj

1. The peel of the Seville orange is quite bitter. To avoid the peel coming into contact with the juice, proceed as follows: Juice 5 to 6 pounds of Seville oranges by first washing and then removing a ring of orange peel from around the middle of each orange. Cut in half. Remove the seeds and press the oranges in a juicer.

2. In a saucepan, bring the brown sugar and water to a boil over high heat. Pour in the Seville orange juice and simmer over medium heat for 20 minutes, stirring occasionally. Remove from heat, cool, pour into a clean, dry bottle, and cork tightly.

3. In a pitcher, mix 1 part syrup, 3 parts water, and 2 ice cubes per person. Stir with a spoon and serve well chilled. Decorate with orange leaves or blossoms. *Nush-e-Jan!*

Rhubarb Syrup

2 pounds rhubarb (about 2 cups
    rhubarb juice)
2 cups water
3 cups brown sugar
2 tablespoons lime juice

Makes 1 pint
Preparation time: 35 minutes
Cooking time: 30 minutes

Sharbat-e rivas

1. Wash and cut the rhubarb into ½-inch pieces. Process in a juicer.

2. Bring the water and brown sugar to a boil in a saucepan. Add the rhubarb juice and lime juice and boil for 20 minutes over medium heat, stirring occasionally.

3. Allow to cool. Pour the syrup into a clean, dry bottle; cork tightly.

4. In a pitcher, mix 1 part syrup, 3 parts water, and 2 ice cubes per person. Stir with a spoon and serve well chilled. *Nush-e-Jan!*

Variation: In a saucepan, bring the brown sugar and 4 cups water to a boil. Tie up the rhubarb pieces in cheesecloth. Place the cheesecloth in the sugar and water and simmer over medium heat for 30 minutes, or until the syrup thickens. Remove the cheesecloth and its contents, pour the syrup into a clean, dry bottle, and cork tightly. Serve as in step 4 above.

Rose Water Syrup

2½ cups water
4 cups sugar
¼ cup fresh lime juice
½ cup rose water

Makes 1 pint
Preparation time: 5 minutes
Cooking time: 20 minutes

شربت گل محمدی

Sharbat-e gol-e Mohammadi

1. Bring water and sugar to a boil in a saucepan. Simmer for 10 minutes. Add the lime juice and rose water and cook 10 minutes longer, stirring occasionally.

2. Remove the pan from heat and allow to cool. Pour the syrup into a clean, dry bottle; cork tightly.

3. In a pitcher, mix 1 part syrup, 3 parts water, and 2 ice cubes per person. Stir with a spoon and serve well chilled. *Nush-e-Jan!*

Vinegar Syrup

6 cups sugar
2 cups water
1½ cups wine vinegar
4 sprigs fresh mint
1 cucumber, peeled and grated

Garnish
Lime slices
Sprigs of mint

Makes 1 pint
Preparation time: 10 minutes
Cooking time: 35 minutes

شربت سکنجبین

Sharbat-e sekanjebin

1. Bring the sugar and water to a boil in a saucepan. Simmer for 10 minutes over medium heat, stirring occasionally, until sugar has thoroughly dissolved.

2. Add the vinegar and boil 15 to 20 minutes longer over medium heat, until a thick syrup forms. Remove the saucepan from heat.

3. Wash the mint sprigs and pat dry. Add them to the syrup. Allow to cool. Remove the mint and pour the syrup into a clean, dry bottle. Cork tightly.

4. In a pitcher, mix 1 part syrup, 3 parts water, and 2 ice cubes per person. Add the cucumber and stir well. Pour into individual glasses and decorate each with a slice of lime and a sprig of fresh mint. Serve well chilled. *Nush-e-Jan!*

Candied Orange Peel

6 oranges
3 cups sugar
3 cups water

Makes about 3 cups

Pust-e porteqal-e shirin

1. Scrub and wash the oranges. Peel thin layers with a peeler and leave the pith on the orange; save the oranges for a fruit salad or juice.

2. Cut the orange peel into slivers of desired length.

3. Place the slivers in a large saucepan and cover with water. Bring to a boil, reduce heat, and cook for 10 minutes over medium heat. Drain in a colander.

4. Place the orange peel back in the saucepan. Add 3 cups sugar and 3 cups water. Bring to a boil, reduce heat to medium and simmer for 20 minutes. Drain and store in a plastic bag in the refrigerator. Use as needed.

Removing Bitterness from Eggplants

Preparation time: 25 minutes

Talkhi gereftan-e bademjan

Method 1: Peel and cut the eggplants into slices of desired thickness and length. Place the eggplant slices in a colander, and place the colander in the sink. Sprinkle the eggplants with water and then with 2 tablespoons salt. Let stand for 20 minutes. The salt will draw out the bitter, black juices from the eggplants. Rinse eggplants with cold water and pat dry.

Method 2: Soak the sliced eggplants in a large container full of cold water with 2 tablespoons salt for 20 minutes. Drain, rinse with cold water, and pat dry.

Hot Fava Beans in the Pod

با قلی پخته

Baqala pokhteh

Hot fava beans, *baqala pokhteh*, are a popular snack, and vendors are a familiar sight in Iranian towns and cities, much like chestnut vendors in winter in New York. *Baqala pokhteh* is usually prepared with fresh fava beans in the pod. Traditionally, the fava beans are boiled with salt, water, and vinegar, then sprinkled with angelica powder (*gol-par*) before serving. For making this snack at home use 2 pounds of fresh fava beans in the pod or 1 pound of frozen fava beans. Wash them and place them in a large pot, add 8 cups of water and 2 tablespoons of salt. Cover and cook for 1 hour over medium heat (if using frozen fava beans without pods, cook for 35 minutes, or until tender). Drain and transfer to a platter, sprinkle with vinegar and then with angelica powder (*gol-par*). These fava beans make a wonderful winter afternoon snack or appetizer. *Nush-e-Jan!*

Baked Beetroots

لبوتنوری

Labu-ye tanuri

Hot beetroot, or *labu*, is a popular snack and its vendors are also a familiar sight in Iranian cities. *Labu* is usually prepared with sweet fresh beets in season. Traditionally, the beetroots are roasted in a *tanur*, or bread oven, and then peeled and sliced before serving. Alternatively, they can be cooked in an oven. Place the beetroots, unpeeled, in an ovenproof baking dish. Cover them with water and bake for 2 to 3 hours at 350°F, depending on their size. Turn them over occasionally; add more warm water if necessary, and cook until tender. Or steam them for about one hour in a steamer or until tender. Peel and slice the beetroots. If you desire, place in a platter, add 2 cups drained yogurt and 2 tablespoons sugar, and mix lightly to avoid the yogurt becoming red. *Nush-e Jan!*

MY MOTHER'S CLASSIFICATION OF "HOT" AND "COLD" FOODS

People are considered to have "hot" and "cold" natures, as does each type of food. This concept has nothing to do with the temperature or the spice and pepper content of the food; it is a system particular unto itself. For Persians, it is essential for persons with "hot" natures to eat "cold" foods and vice versa, in order to create a balanced diet.

Recipes in this book present a balanced diet by combining the opposing elements of "hot" and "cold." It should be noted that both the the pharmacological and culinary qualities of the spices also play an important role.

Meat

Beef, veal	cold
Duck	hot
Hen	hot
Lamb	hot
Red snapper	hot
All other fish	cold
Rooster	cold
Turkey	cold

Vegetables

Beets	cold
Cabbage	cold
Cardoons	cold
Carrots	hot
Cauliflower	cold
Celery	cold
Corn	hot
Cucumber	cold
Eggplants	cold
Garlic	hot
Grape leaves	cold
Green beans	cold
Green peas	cold
Green peppers	hot
Lettuce	cold
Mushrooms	hot
Okra	hot
Onions	hot
Potatoes	cold
Pumpkins	cold
Rhubarb	cold
Shallots	hot
Spinach	cold
Tomatoes	cold
Turnips	cold

Cereals and Beans

Barley	cold
Barley flour	cold
Chickpeas	hot
Cornstarch	hot
Kidney beans	cold
Lentils	cold
Mung beans	hot
Pinto beans	cold
Rice	cold
Wheat flour	hot
Yellow fava beans	cold
Yellow split peas	hot

Fruits and Nuts

Almonds	hot
Apples	hot
Apricots	cold
Barberries	cold
Dates	hot
Figs	hot
Grapefruit	cold
Mangoes	hot
Nectarines	cold
Oranges	cold
Peaches	cold
Pears	neutral
Pistachios	hot
Prunes	cold
Quinces	hot
Raisins and grapes	hot
Sweet melon	hot
Tart cherries	cold
Walnuts	hot
Watermelon	cold
Persian limes	cold

Herbs

Bay leaf	hot
Chives	hot
Coriander	cold
Dill weed	hot
Fenugreek	hot
Garden angelica	hot
Marjoram	hot
Mint	hot
Parsley	hot
Tarragon	hot

Spices

Cardamom	hot
Cinnamon	hot
Cloves	hot
Cumin seed	hot
Curry powder	hot
Ginger	hot
Nigella seed	hot
Nutmeg	hot
Pepper	hot
Saffron	hot
Salt	hot
Sumac	cold
Turmeric	hot
Vanilla	hot

Other

Coffee	cold
Eggs	hot
Feta cheese	neutral
Honey	hot
Lemon juice	cold
Milk	cold
Persian pickles	hot
Pomegranate paste	cold
Rose water	hot
Sugar	cold
Tamarind	cold
Tea	neutral
Tomato paste	cold
Sour grape juice	cold
Vinegar	hot
Whey	hot
Yogurt	cold

E Q U I V A L E N T   M E A S U R E S

U.S. Liquid	Equivalents	Metric
1 teaspoon	60 drops	5 ml
1 tablespoon	3 teaspoons	15 ml
2 tablespoons	1 fluid ounce	30 ml
4 tablespoons	¼ cup	60 ml
5½ tablespoons	⅓ cup	80 ml
8 tablespoons	½ cup	120 ml
10⅔ tablespoons	⅔ cup	160 ml
12 tablespoons	¾ cup	180 ml
16 tablespoons	1 cup or 8 ounces	240 ml
1 cup	½ pint or 8 fluid ounces	240 ml
2 cups	1 pint	480 ml
1 pint	16 ounces	480 ml
2 pints	1 quart	960 ml (approx. 1 ltr)
2 quarts	½ gallon	
4 quarts	1 gallon	3.8 liters

Weight

1 ounce	16 drams	28 grams
1 pound	16 ounces	454 grams
1 pound	2 cups liquid	454 grams
1 kilo	2.20 pounds	1,000 grams

Temperature

Fahrenheit	200	225	250	275	300	325	350	375	400	425	450	475
Gas Mark			1	2	3	4	5	6	7	8	9	
Centigrade	93	110	130	140	150	170	180	190	200	220	230	240

PERSIAN KITCHEN INGREDIENTS

Whenever possible, use fresh herbs, beans, fruit, and nuts, which are more and more commonly available in most supermarkets. Below is a list of some essential ingredients that should be kept in your pantry in dried form. Make the syrups, jams, and pickles from time to time, store them in jars, and use as needed.

DRIED HERBS
Basil—*Reyhan*
Bay leaf—*Barg-e bu*
Chives—*Tareh*
Coriander leaves; also called cilantro or Chinese parsley—*Gishniz*
Dill weed—*Shivid*
Dried Persian lime powder—*Gard-e-limu-omani*
Fenugreek—*Shanbalileh*
Garden angelica—*Gol-par*
Mint—*Na'na*
Summer savory—*Marzeh*
Tarragon—*Tarkhun*
Whole dried Persian limes—*Limu-omani*

DRIED BEANS
Barley—*Jow*
Chickpeas—*Nokhod*
Green fava beans or lima beans—*Baqali*
Kidney beans—*Lubia qermez*
Lentils—*Adas*
Pinto beans—*Lubia chiti*
Yellow fava beans—*Baqali-e zard*
Yellow split peas—*Lapeh*

SPICES
A mixture of 4–8 ground spices—*Advieh*
Cardamom—*Hel*
Cinnamon—*Darchin*
Cloves—*Mikhak*

Cumin seed—*Zireh*
Curry powder—*Kari*
Ginger—*Zanjebil*
Nigella seeds (black caraway seeds)—*Siah daneh*
Nutmeg—*Jowz-e hendi*
Saffron—*Za'feran*
Sumac—*Somaq*
Turmeric—*Zardchubeh*
Vanilla—*Vanil*

OTHER
Garlic—*Sir*
Lemon juice—*Ablimu*
Long-grain rice (Basmati)—*Berenj*
Olive oil—*Roghan zeytun*
Onions—*Piaz*
Persian pickles—*Torshi*
Quince—*Beh*
Rose water—*Golab*
Sour grape juice—*Ab ghureh*
Vinegar—*Serkeh*
Whey—*Kashk*

PASTES
Essence of grape—*Shireh-ye angur*
Pomegranate paste—*Rob-e-anar*
Seville orange paste—*Rob-e narenj*
Tomato paste—*Rob-e gojeh farangi*

SYRUPS AND JAMS
Orange peel—*Pust-e porteqal*
Vinegar syrup—*Sekanjebine*
Tart cherry preserve—*Moraba-ye albalu*

DRIED FRUITS, FLOWERS AND NUTS
Almond slivers—*Khalal-e-badam*
Apricots—*Gheisi*
Barberries—*Zereshk*
Dates—*Khorma*
Orange blossom—*Bahar narenj*
Pistachio slivers—*Khalal-e-pesteh*
Pistachios—*Pesteh*
Prunes—*Alu*
Quince blossom—*Gol-e Beh*
Raisins—*Keshmesh*
Rose petals—*Gole-e sorkh*
Seville orange—*Narenj*
Tamarind—*Tamr*
Walnuts—*Gerdu*

SPECIALTY STORES & RESTAURANTS

Arizona

Apadana Restaurant
Tempe
(602) 945-5900

International Foods Wholesale
Tempe
(602) 894-2442

California

Alvand Market
Costa Mesa
(714) 545-7177

Anoush Deli & Grocery
Hollywood
(213) 465-4062

Apadana Market & Deli
Westlake Village
(818) 991-1268

Bazjian's Grocery, Inc.
Hollywood
(213) 663-1503

Caspian Persian Cuisine
Sunnyvale
(408) 248-6332

Caspian Restaurant
Irvine
(714) 651-8454

Colbeh Iran
Reseda
(818) 344-2300

Danaian's Bakery
Hollywood
(213) 664-8842

Darya Restaurant
Orange
(714) 921-2773

Downtown Kabab
Los Angeles
(213) 612-0222

Farid Restaurant
Los Angeles
(213) 622-0808

Shahrzad Restaurant
Los Angeles
(310) 470-3242

Golestan Restaurant
Los Angeles
(213) 470-3867

Hatam Restaurant
San Rafael
(415) 454-8888

Iran Markets, Inc., #1
Reseda
(818) 342-9753

Jilla's Gourmet Catering
Berkeley
(510) 938-6537

Hafez Restaurant
San Francisco
(415) 563-7456

Kabob House Restaurant
Anaheim
(714) 991-6262

Karoun Market
Hollywood
(213) 665-7237

Kashmiri Grocery
Hawthorne
(213) 978-1927

Kasra Restaurant
San Francisco
(415) 752-1101

Khatoon
San Diego
(619) 459-4016

Lavash Corporation
of America
Los Angeles
(213) 663-5249

Mahtab Market
Rancho Palos Verdes
(213) 833-6026

Massoud Restaurant
Los Angeles
(213) 748-1768

Maykadeh Restaurant
San Francisco
(415) 362-8286

Paradise Restaurant
Mt. View
(415) 968-5949

Pars Market
Los Angeles
(213) 859-8125

Pars Market
San Diego
(619) 566-7277

Pars Restaurant
San Bruno
(415) 871-5151

Persian Center Bazar
San Jose
(408) 241-3700

Raffi's Place #1
Glendale
(818) 241-9960

Ramsar Market
Los Angeles
(213) 651-1601

Rose's Restaurant
Canoga Park
(818) 716-5222

Saam Middle East
Restaurant
Pasadena
(818) 793-8496

Salar Restaurant
Glendale
(818) 500-8661

Samirami's Market
San Francisco
(415) 824-6555

Sepah Market
Irvine
(714) 559-4510

Shahrzad International
Market
Santa Ana
(714) 850-0808

Shamshiri Restaurant
Hollywood
(213) 469-8434

Shamshiri Restaurant
Northridge
(818) 885-7846

Shamshiri Restaurant
Glendale
(818) 246-9541

Shamshiri Restaurant
San Jose
(408) 998-0122

Sholeh Restaurant
Los Angeles
(310) 470-9131

Sultani Restaurant
Hollywood
(213) 876-3389

Tehran Market
Santa Monica
(310) 393-6719

Connecticut

Sharzad Grocery
Stamford
(203) 323-5363

District of Columbia

International Market
& Deli
(202) 293-0499

Kolbeh Restaurant
(202) 342-2000

Taverna Market
(202) 333-1972

Nakeysa Restaurant
(202) 337-6500

University Market Place
(202) 667-2206

Florida

Shiraz Food Market
Miami
(305) 264-8282

Georgia

1001 Nights Restaurant
Atlanta
(404) 851-9566

Shahrzad International
Atlanta
(404) 843-0549

Illinois

Arya Food Imports
Chicago
(312) 878-2092

International Foods
Chicago
(312) 478-8643

Middle East Trading
Chicago
(312) 262-2848

Middle Eastern Bakery
 & Grocer
Chicago
(312) 561-2224

Sahar Meat & Grocery
Chicago
(312) 583-7772

Maryland

E. & I. International
Rockville
(301) 984-8287

International House
Rockville
(301) 279-2121

Moby Dick Cafe
Maryland
(301) 654-1838

Paradise
Bethesda
(310) 907-7500

Persepolis Restaurant
Bethesda
(301) 656-9339

Villa Market
Chevy Chase
(301) 951-0062

Yas Bakery
 & Confectionery
Rockville
(301) 762-5416

Yekta Middle Eastern
 Grocery
Rockville
(301) 984-1190

Massachusetts

Ararat Restaurant
Watertown
(617) 924-4100

Michigan

International Market
Livonia
(313) 522-2220

Minnesota
Caspian Bistro
Minneapolis
(612) 623-1113

Nevada

Middle Eastern Bazar
Las Vegas
(702) 731-6030

New Jersey

Amir Bakery
Paterson
(201) 345-5030

New York

Bahar Market
Great Neck
(516) 466-2222

Caravan Restaurant
New York
(212) 262-2021

Colbeh Restaurant
Great Neck
(516) 466-8181

International Food
 Market
Roslyn Heights
(516) 625-5800

International Grocery Store
New York
(212) 279-5514

Kababi-e-Nader
New York
(212) 683-4833

Khazar Restaurant
New York
(212) 787-9200

Persepolis Restaurant
New York
(212) 535-1100

North Carolina

University Pantry Deli
Charlotte
(704) 549-9156

Ohio

Aladdin's Middle
 East Bakery
Cleveland
(216) 861-0317

Oregon

International Food Bazar
Portland
(503) 228-1960

Rose International Foods
Beaverton
(503) 646-7673

Texas

Darband Kababi
Houston
(713) 975-8350

Super Vanak
 International Food
Houston
(713) 952-7676

Virginia

Assal Market
Vienna
(703) 281-2248

Bahar Restaurant
Vienna
(703) 242-2427

Bread & Kabab
Falls Church
(703) 845-2900

Cafe Rose
Falls Church
(703) 532-1700

Moustache Cafe #2
Tysons Corner
(703) 893-1100

Shamshiri
Tysons Corner
(703) 448-8883

Washington State

Pars Market
Bellevue
(206) 641-5265

Rooz Super Market
 & Deli
Seattle
(206) 363-8639

INDEX OF RECIPES

Meat, Chicken, and Fish

Rice

CREDITS & ACKNOWLEDGMENTS

Photographs
Serge Ephraim, La Colle sur Loup, France: all photographs except as listed below
Fred J. Maroon, Washington, DC: cover photograph
Mohammad Batmanglij, Washington, DC: page 48
Max Hirshfeld, Washington, DC: page 108

Presentation
Thierry Jeaneret, Chef at the Belles Rives Hotel in Juan les Pins, aided the author in the presentation.

Recipe Testing
Parvaneh Matini tested the recipes with her knowledge and expertise of authentic Persian cuisine. Catherine Evans, a culinary educator at the Smithsonian, tested the recipes for preparation in an American kitchen.

Persian Calligraphy
Amir Hossein Tabnak, Washington, D.C., and Bijan Bijani, Tehran

I would like to thank both Serge and Thierry for their help in many weeks of non-stop Franco-Persian cooking and photography. Though the night life and jazz in Georgetown beckoned, they kept working frequently past midnight to get the right shot. I would also like to thank George Constable, our friend and neighbor, for his invaluable help and editorial insight.

I wish to thank my sister Ezat, who helped me with devotion, and my sister Shirin, who was my assistant throughout this project. During the photography many friends and neighbors brought out their Persian treasures; in particular I wish to thank my neighbor Farideh Ardalan for so generously lending me her family heirlooms. I would also like to thank Ehsan for lending me her by now famous plates, and the Appalachian Spring in Georgetown for allowing me to use their dishes.

As usual my favorite local grocers came through and found me everything I needed. Special thanks go to Richard, Maroun, Bill and Eddie at Neams, and Dan at Dean and Deluca, Georgetown. Debbie Jacomet kept us supplied with fresh herbs and difficult-to-find fruits and vegetables such as quinces and quince blossoms.

Thanks are also due to Gerry and Joanne of Editype for their careful and thorough preparation of the type, and to Bill Henry at Mage for its production.